BLACK LIVERPOOL

THE EARLY HISTORY OF BRITAIN'S OLDEST BLACK COMMUNITY 1730-1918

By

Ray Costello

The City of Liverpool

British Library Cataloguing in Publication Data. A Catalogue record of this book is available from the British Library.

ISBN 1 873245 07 6

DISCLAIMER

The author has made every attempt to credit all references and acknowledge all sources of both visual and printed material.

First published 2001 by Picton Press (Liverpool) 14 Appin Road, Birkenhead CH41 9HH

Printed by Birkenhead Press Ltd. 14 Appin Road, Birkenhead CH41 9HH

PUBLISHERS NOTE

Views and conclusions stated in this publication are those of the author and those he has interviewed. The publishers do not accept any responsibility for these views, conclusions or for the accuracy of information contained in the book.

Every effort has been made to trace copyright holders of illustrative materials. We apologise if we have inadvertently omitted any acknowledgement.

JACKET DESIGN CONSULTANTS:
Douglas Harker, Danny Anderson and Kathryn Dubber

FRONT COVER:
Top: Left to right - Emily Orgill, Edward and Harriet James
Bottom: Marcus Bailey and an un-named soldier, Soraya Bond, Gemma Bond; great-great granddaughters of Edward and Harriet James, immediately above (120 years separate these photographs of the same Liverpool Black family)

BACK COVER:
An artists impression of a Black Loyalist soldier

This book is dedicated to my mother,
Edith Mary Costello

BLACK LIVERPOOL

THE EARLY HISTORY OF BRITAIN'S OLDEST BLACK COMMUNITY
1730-1918

CONTENTS

Background image: William James was born in Liverpool in the 1870s. A sailor all his life, he was buried at sea.

INTRODUCTION

Many people in Britain are unaware of the presence of a continuous Black British community dating back more than two and a half centuries. I first became conscious of the need for a written history of the Liverpool Black Community when I was a schoolboy in Liverpool District 8, now popularly known through the media as Toxteth. At school I became aware that the "People of Many Lands" lessons about people of African descent were not always about the black people I met in the streets in the course of my daily life and not always of direct relevance to my black schoolmates. Many black people I knew, including some of my relatives, were, indeed, recent settlers from former British colonies, but it seemed that all black people were presented as a people living overseas, with different cultures and lifestyles - belonging elsewhere and un-British. This begged the question, "Who are our local black people, proud of their racial origins, but born in this country for many generations and British in every respect in terms of language, religions and culture?" Now that I know, the first step, it seems to me, is to tell the rest of the world who they are, and when and how they came to be here.

It was the Swann Report on education, "Education for All" in 1985, which first coined the phrase "Liverpool Blacks", inadvertently providing a name for a people who always knew who they were themselves, but were largely unheard of, at least as an ancient community, to the rest of the country. The old Liverpool Black population dealt centuries ago with all the difficulties of language and original religion or culture that usually beset immigrants and any isolation has never been voluntary. In spite of this, the community still faces racism, and, more than simply overt prejudice, the omission of all traces of their existence from the history books, as though they do not exist or have never existed.

It was with this particular deficiency in mind that this book has been written in the hope that some contribution might be made to correcting that omission; filling the gap by adding faces and personalities to the ancestors of a forgotten section of society and, in doing so, throwing some light upon the current situation of black Liverpudlians and all black people of African descent in Great Britain. There are many eminent early black Liverpudlians who are totally unknown to black or white, but this book does not concentrate entirely upon 'great' men and women, however potentially useful models they may be to young black people. It is also testimony to those other early black Liverpudlians whose lives may have seemed undramatic or mundane, but are nevertheless no less heroic in dealing with the daily struggle of life in what were often hard times for black people.

Anyone who has lived in Liverpool for any length of time will be aware of a local black community popularly described in terms of being vaguely 'old'. The question often asked is 'Just how old?' One of the difficulties of writing a history of the Liverpool Black Community is that as this area of research is relatively new, as soon as students of black history settle for a particular date for the beginning of the Black Community, some new information arises to push back that date even further. This book simply represents the present state of research and will hopefully encourage other students to carry the search further.

This book is more than just the early history of the Liverpool Black Community. Serious issues of national identity are raised here. It has often been said that, as the oldest black community in Great Britain, Liverpool is a paradigm for other

British cities with a similar population of racial minorities; a model and example for other cities with a future British-born black population to add and widen the existing variety of people that make up the British people. Also, it is important to remember that this is not just the history of the oldest section of the Black Community; it is the history of the roots of a continuous community that recent black settlers have chosen as their own, enriching that established community, for there is no differentiation between the old and the new. The Liverpool Black Community is already no longer an isolated anomaly in social terms. Many immigrants who came to other parts of Britain from the New Commonwealth following World War II are already grandparents, their descendants well into the second generation of U.K.- born black people. Those earliest Liverpool Black Settlers deserve to have their story told.

This book was written as a response to increasing pressure from both the Black Community and teachers to fill a void in British (and local) history. Even the cause of multicultural and anti-racist education has done little to answer the gap in the curriculum, as often the route taken is an essentially purist one of nationalities and overseas cultures. The difficulty is that if the descendants of early black settlers have lost their diverse cultures, languages and religions, they are not always conceived of as being a people, with the danger of not being seen as people at all, instead of a group deserving to have their own rich history recorded. This need, unfulfilled up to the present, has been underlined by the Gifford Report on racial disadvantage in Liverpool, "Loosen The Shackles" (Karia Press, 1989), which pinpointed the need for an understanding and knowledge of the history of the black community, supported by other local and national publications, including Stephen Small's "Racialised Relations in Liverpool - A Contemporary Anomaly" (in "New Community", vol. 17, no. 4, 1991).

Writing the history of a community whose existence in Great Britain has been largely unacknowledged has not been easy. The evidence is scattered, frequently a single line in a seemingly unpromising document. An example found in this book is the inclusion of a letter written by an eighteenth century African prince who was educated in Liverpool, a true voice of a black student from the past found in an unlikely nineteenth century book on Liverpool privateers. This book could only have been written "from the inside", so to speak, and some of the source material is primary in its truest sense, namely the verbal testimony of members of the Liverpool Black Community, easily born out later by documentary evidence. Other sources have included contemporary newspapers and magazines, and both modern and contemporary secondary sources. The precaution of testing and balancing all material with the testimony of black writers and commentators has also been taken.

ACKNOWLEDGEMENTS

I will never be able to thank enough those people who have selflessly given their help in producing this book. First and foremost must surely be the heads and representatives of Liverpool Black families for whom I have the utmost respect.

They are:

George and Annie Quarless, Maxine Eyo, Ray Kadiri, Jimmy Kadiri, Jimmy Kadiri (Jnr.), Araba Bond, Edwin Bond, Yasmin Bond, Maria O'Reilly, Remon Nowell, Brenda Freeman, Lenford White, Eric Lynch, Agnes Brew, Kenneth Brew, Joan von Linstow, Kim Iniabere, Dorothy Kuya, Solomon Bassey, Grace Wilkie, Wes Wilkie, David Abdullah, Donna Palmer, Linda Loy, Vincent Clarke, Beverley Clarke, Laurence Westgarth, Carol Darby, Russell Tago, Norman Tagoe, Lilian Bader, Margaret Othick, Susan Sweeting, Mary Jane Sweeting, Hazel Lopez, Rachel Freeman, Irene Cole.

I am also indebted to the following friends and allies who have supported and given practical help:

Anne Wright of Liverpool City Council, Anne Whittaker of National Museums and Galleries on Merseyside, Philippa Gregory, authoress of "A Respectable Trade", Julie Gregson of the Local History Collection, Battersea Library, the artist Paul Clarkson, Eddie Conway, Frank Anti and Lucy Hodson of Churches Action for Racial Equality (C.A.R.E.), Harold and Joyce Culling of Liverpool and South Lancashire Family History Society, Scouse Press, Jeffrey Green, John Latham, Tony Glennon, Peter Price, Douglas Harker, Billy McIlhatton, Laurence Weston, Dave Corker, Roger Sims of Manx National Heritage, James E. Cowden and John O. C. Duffy, authors of "The Elder Dempster Fleet History 1852-1985" and publishers Mallet and Bell, Janet Sykes and Sarah Morley of Pearson Education for their efforts to find the unfindable source of an eighteenth century illustration which appears in this book. The British Broadcasting Corporation Television (BBC).

Finally, this book would never have appeared in print without those people prepared to make a leap of faith by both financing and promoting it in other ways. These are John and Jean Emmerson of Countyvise (Picton Press), David Stoker of Liverpool City Libraries Record Office and his excellent staff, John Murphy and Elaine Rees of Dingle/Granby/Toxteth Education Action Zone, Janet Dugdale and Garry Morris of National Museums and Galleries on Merseyside and Gloria Hyatt of Elimu Academy.

THE GROWTH OF THE LIVERPOOL BLACK COMMUNITY

This is the story of an invisible people.

The Liverpool Black Community has been described as the oldest in Europe, though other, even older, black settlements have existed in Britain for at least five centuries[1]. What distinguishes the Liverpool Black Community from those of other cities such as Bristol and London is its continuity, some black Liverpudlians being able to trace their roots in Liverpool for as many as ten generations. There are black communities in present-day Bristol and London, but there have been gaps, communities dying out only to rise again at a later date.

Although the Liverpool Black Community owes its origin to the Slave Trade, many of the myths and assumptions about the first black settlers will be dispelled in this book. During the course of the eighteenth century, the rise of Liverpool from an obscure seaport to one of the richest trading centres in Europe also saw its emergence as a centre for the education of early black students and the home of a free black community drawn from many sources. In later chapters, the names, faces and personalities will be added to these early forgotten Black British, lost in the mists of time.

Some black families have existed in Liverpool almost as long as the Huguenots - French protestant refugees who settled in this country during the seventeenth and eighteenth centuries to escape persecution - the asylum seekers of their time. Huguenot families settling in the North-West in towns such as Prescot and Widnes are now considered as being indisputably British - even English. Britain is an island peopled by successive waves of immigrants, the majority having been gradually accepted into the mainstream of British life. Some groups, such as Jewish settlers, have had great difficulty in becoming assimilated owing to religion. In the case of people of African descent, skin colour has been the overriding factor, a characteristic impossible to change, convert or compromise, and, ironically when the hidden character of the present Liverpool Black Community is considered, obviously far more noticeable because of its very visibility.

The Liverpool Black Community is an example of a distinct people having the appearance of almost complete invisibility for more than two hundred years. Although recognised as being virtually an homogenous people in a few official documents, such as the Swann Report which included a separate chapter on "Liverpool Blacks", this community has remained separate but part of the British Nation, scant evidence being found by the casual visitor of the existence of this old community in terms of either records or physical presence in shops in the City's central business district.

This, then, is their story.

THE SLAVE TRADE

The Liverpool Black Community is both a direct and indirect result of the Slave Trade. Following the mid-eighteenth century, Liverpool steadily overtook Bristol, her main rival in the Slave Trade.[2] London, the other contender, had almost given up the Slave Trade by 1720, the year of the South Sea disaster.[3] In 1764, Bristol cleared only thirty-two ships for Africa whilst Liverpool cleared seventy-four, having more than a half of

BELL TOWN BEACH, DUALA, ESTUARY OF CAMEROONS RIVER

Drawn by Sir H. H. Johnston

◀ **A trading hulk lies off the West African Coast. The daily trading in slaves was sometimes done from stations like the one shown in the picture. A ship is seen standing off shore ready to receive slaves ferried out by canoe.**

the British African Trade.[4] By 1795, Liverpool had the monopoly of five-eighths of the European Slave Trade.[5]

African slaves were sold in the Caribbean and the Americas through what is known as the 'Triagular Trade', which began with ships setting sail from Liverpool, buying, or, in some cases, capturing young Africans on the West African coast. They would then embark upon the infamous 'middle passage', sailing from the African coast to the West Indies, as often as not Barbados, one of the prime destinations. It was during this middle passage that most of the fatalities occurred, as slaves were packed tight in appalling conditions and ships' captains were not above throwing slaves overboard in order to collect the insurance if it was found that the price of slaves had dropped in the Caribbean. 'Brown sugar' was the commodity usually entered in the log book when this happened. When the ships arrived in the West Indies and the slaves were auctioned to the plantation owners, the captains would then load up with a cargo of goods and commodities from the Caribbean which could be sold back in Britain. It was this trade in human beings that led to the first black people arriving in Liverpool as part of the to and fro of commerce, as ships' captains would often bring back personal black servants and slaves, only to sell them on at some point to the township's wealthy merchants anxious to show their new status by owning what was to become highly fashionable black servants and slaves, the distinction between free black and those in bondage often being slight.

One glimmer of hope and evidence of humanity at this time was the fact that within a very few years of the first slaver sailing from Liverpool in 1699, the principle of a man or woman being owned by another was being challenged by enlightened individuals; powerless at the beginning, but steadily gaining ground. As early as 1706, it was stated in court that a black person was like any other human being in that he or she could not be inherited in a will like goods or other chattels. A little later, the same judge, Chief Justice Holt, claimed that a slave was free as soon as he arrives in England. This was easier said than done and it was to be at least a century before this law was to be taken seriously. In 1729, the Yorke and Talbot ruling appeared to reverse Holt's decision, to be thrown out in turn by Lord Justice Henley, who reaffirmed the principle that a slave was free as soon as he sets foot in England. The famous Mansfield Judgement of 1772 was one of the last important steps in the struggle leading to Abolition by disallowing slaves to be taken from England against their will.

Throughout this book, the Slave Trade will be seen to brood over the whole period as the raison d'être of black settlement in England. The stark numerical figures and diagrams of slave ships usually seen in books on the Slave Trade are replaced by named individuals in this book; to remind readers that the trade was one of human souls. The names of the descendants of slaves are never those of their original family in their countries of origin, but in many cases they have brought more honour to those names than the slave owners whose names they inherited ever did. The original experience of black slaves in the West Indies and the Americas generally was designed to deprive them of their own language, seen as a way of facilitating rebellion; a family life, as emotional ties through marriages or even permanent relationships made the sale of individuals more difficult; culture, art forms and even music, being seen as a means of communication possibly only understood by the slave at their master's expense as were religion, and education. The plight of blacks of the diaspora was not confined to slaves. A law passed in Georgia in 1829 stated that if any slave, free black or any white person taught a black person to read or write, blacks would be punished by a fine and whipping. The white person would also be punished with a fine of $500 and imprisonment at the discretion of the Court.

The Slave Trade itself ended in 1807, but the idea of producing a totally compliant black population devoid of initiative, will, dignity and skills considered superfluous to the needs of their owners did not end with the final Abolition of Slavery in 1834 (in British Territories, though black slavery was to linger on until the 1860s in the United states and as late as 1888 in Brazil). Following Emancipation, black people of the diaspora were, to a large extent, left unprovided for in a society still reluctant to allow them any prestige in their black identity a situation yet to be resolved, even amongst the secondary diaspora in what, as a result of the earlier brainwashing procedure, came to be known as

the "Mother Country". For the human beings used as a commodity, the grim reality of slavery stood in stark contrast to the healthy balance sheets of Liverpool traders involved in their sale.

During the eighteenth century, Britain's African trade formed part of the Atlantic network linking her with the Americas and West African coast, dealing in ivory, gold, wax, dyeing woods and slaves; the necessities of life in the New World[6]. Early coastal forts such as Anomabu, Cape Coast Castle and other British settlements carried out the day to day trade, British traders soon finding the coastal peoples of West Africa to be by no means the naive aboriginals they had possibly hoped for. Soon the coastal peoples were acting as middlemen between the Europeans and various African nations of the African interior.

BLACK STUDENTS

The first myth to explode is the origin of the early black settlers. Although the Slave Trade might have been the cause of black people settling in Britain, by no means all black people were slaves or servants. There was a good deal to be gained politically by the British in encouraging overseas scholarship. Other countries, such as France, were deeply involved in trade rivalries in the eighteenth century and it was thought that by offering educational opportunities in Britain, not only would the sons of African chiefs receive an indoctrination favourable to the British viewpoint, but their fathers might hopefully feel some gratitude, both strengthening the political bonds between the two countries. The other European powers had much the same idea and often African children were sent to France for the same purpose [8]. Hugh Crow, captain of one of the last slavers to leave Liverpool, commented that, for as long as he could remember, Africans had been encouraged by merchants and ships' captains to send their children to England; the belief being that it consolidated their friendship, added to the security of the traders and, to use his term, "soften their manners" [9] (no doubt he meant to European norms!) Some wily and politically astute rulers hedged their bets and sent a son to each European country!

During the period of the Slave Trade, there was always the danger of would-be students travelling to Liverpool being sold as slaves by unscrupulous ships' captains who considered one sort of black much the same as another. The Nassau Papers of February 22nd, 1799 record -

"On board the sloop "Henry", Cusack, from Africa for this port, captured by the Spanish schooner ,"St. Rosalia", Captain Monase, were two African youths of about twelve years, one named John, the son of King George, and the other, Tom, son of King John Qua Ben, both having extensive domains on the river Gaboon. These youths their fathers committed to the charge of Captain Cusack to be carried to Liverpool, there to be educated. They were both taken from Captain Cusack, to be sold as slaves in spite of all his remonstrances, and at Havannah, he was told by a respectable Spanish merchant that they would not be delivered up." [10]

Captain Cusack, no doubt an honourable man, fought tooth and nail to keep the two African princes from being sold into slavery and obviously did not want accusations levelled at him such as those of the author Boswell, who showed his disgust and anger in print at what he called those 'wretches' who had been entrusted with the care of princes in order to provide them with a European education, only to have them sold in plantations in such islands as Jamaica, where, he knew only too well, the laws did not apply to blacks of any station.[11] Boswell felt that unscrupulous ship's captains were doing it regularly, which begs the question, "how many present-day West Indians are descended from these lost princes?" Dorothy Kuya, Liverpool-born and a life-long activist in the cause of black people of the Diaspora, opened the Africa 2000 Conference in August of that year with -

"Bothers and sisters! I use the term "Brothers and sisters" as black people of the Diaspora often do. The reason we say

◄ A slave auction, by a contempory 18th century illustrator

11

this is that we do not know whether we are or not! We have been torn from Africa, sold in the Caribbean and ended up all over the Western world!"

Dorothy was using "brothers and sisters" in the African sense, various cousins being included. Throughout this book, the personal, familial, relationship between different parts of the black Diaspora; the Caribbean, the Americas, Africa herself and British black people, such as those to be found in Liverpool, will become clear.

African rulers would send their children to be educated in Europe voluntarily, usually under the guardianship of traders or ships' captains. Early African students were educated in Britain both as groups and individuals [12] and during the 1780s there were African children of both sexes in Liverpool and the surrounding area, chiefly from the Windward and Gold Coasts.[13] It was thought that there were generally from fifty to seventy of these children at school in Liverpool (do not forget that Liverpool was quite small at this time), beside those who came to London and Bristol, "to learn good sense and get a good head" as some chiefs expressed it. After receiving a good common school education, they usually returned to Africa, where they would often dress and live out the rest of their lives in the European manner, [14] their countrymen - not yet realising the true cost in terms of the growing dependency and seeds of colonialism - frequently valuing and respecting them on account of their European education.

Not all black students returned to Africa or the West Indies; some chose to stay in the land where they had grown up, adding to the growth of the Liverpool Black Community. This was the beginning of a tradition in Liverpool that would last until the present day. Not the least contribution to the Liverpool Black Community has been later African students, the spiritual and physical descendants of those early sons of African rulers who were originally sent to England for a Western style education, only to settle and find wives and homes here. Links with Africa were strengthened even further by a succession of African students

wishing to complete their education in a place where they would find relatives. Many well-to-do African families felt that if their children had to make the journey to a strange land, where better than Liverpool where friends and relatives already existed? Liverpool was to continue as a focus for black students, drawn by bonds of kinship to the black Liverpool population and later as a safe haven for black students visiting Britain in a worsening social climate for blacks as the 19th century progressed.

This policy of African rulers sending their children to Britain to be educated was to lead to an increase in the black presence in Liverpool and still provides a confusing ingredient insofar as the social class of present-day black families is concerned. Because of the increasing development of negative attitudes towards black people during the nineteenth century, black people of all stations faced rejection in British society; the son of an African king being considered no more than a black person of 'lower station.'[15] This has led to a large degree of intermarriage across the social spectrum among black Liverpudlians; it being considered quite normal for many modern black families in Liverpool to include a variety of social classes - a well educated grandfather who may well have been considered a minor African prince in his country of origin, a West Indian uncle who was a volunteer in the British forces during World War II, an unemployed British-born father and a variety of cousins living on the poverty line. This contrasts considerably with many of their white neighbours, who may have been poor for many generations and often do not present the same variety of social classes within the same family.

During the last quarter of the eighteenth century, black settlers, either as slaves, servants, students of noble descent or the dual heritage children of white plantation owners and African slave women, were both visiting or settling all over Liverpool and the surrounding district. All that was required now was the heart of a distinct black community to be established.

BLACK AMERICAN LOYALISTS

Following World War II, many young women of the Liverpool Black Community found husbands amongst the black G.I.s stationed at the nearby American Camp at Burtonwood, leaving their families to live in what, to them, was a foreign country. Many people would be surprised to learn that this is not the first time black Americans have had an influence upon the Liverpool Black Community. Black Americans could arguably be described as being the founders of the community in terms of large numbers, settling here in Britain by travelling in exactly the opposite direction to Liverpool Black girls in the 1950s. In spite of the growing number of free black students, black slaves and servants in the latter half of the eighteenth century, it was not until the 1780s that any sizable community could

▲ An artist's imprssion of a Black Loyalist Soldier during the War of American Independence. Many settled in Liverpool after the war.

be recognised in Liverpool.

The influx of black Americans came about in this way. During the American War of Independence (1775-1783), some black slaves remained loyal to Britain, lured by the promise of freedom. When the North American Colonies openly rebelled against British rule, Lord Dunmore, the British Royal Governor of Virginia, believed that he had found a way of dealing with the fact of British forces being seriously outnumbered in America by the American rebels at a time when reinforcements took a long time to arrive by ship from Britain. In November of 1775, a proclamation was issued offering freedom to all slaves who deserted their American rebel masters. White Americans who remained loyal to Britain were not seriously threatened as most of the slaveholding regions were in rebel areas, but the general plan was to cause white rebel slaveowners some consternation at the idea of having a potential enemy in their own household, namely their own domestic slaves![16] Those slaves who accepted the offer were formed into black regiments with white officers, but as the war progressed, both sides were using black troops. At first, they were used in non-combat roles - cooks, stretcher-bearers and ammunition carriers - because of the fear of black slaves with guns, but, as in all of America's future wars, the need for cannon-fodder caused black soldiers to be eventually involved in direct fighting. [17] To some, the idea of a black redcoat may seem an anomaly, but the truth is that the British 'thin red line' was sometimes black.

Could the amateur American rebel army hold out against one of the world's greatest powers? Did they have even the remotest chance of success? In 1781, it seemed that the impossible happened. The seemingly invincible British army surrendered at Yorktown to what was felt back home to be a raggle-taggle band of country bumpkins - the American Continental Army! This left the British with not only the problem of evacuating their own troops, but their black allies. Following the war, many of these "black loyalist"

▲ As the War of American Independence progressed, black troops were used in a direct military role on both sides, as this action picture based on a painting "The Battle of Cowpens" by William Ranney of South Carolina shows.

ex-servicemen were now forced to seek a new life in British-held possessions such as Canada (Nova Scotia particularly), having freedom but little else. When the British left Charleston, they took with them 5,000 black soldiers, followed by several thousands more when they left Savannah and New York.[18]

Those who chose to come to Britain herself helped to swell the numbers of the black poor. In London particularly, many poor blacks were reduced to begging on the streets after failing to find employment, a condition that drew the attention of a group of gentlemen, bankers, merchants and Members of Parliament, who, calling themselves the 'Committee for the Relief of the Black Poor' under the philanthropist Jonas Hanway, raised funds for food, clothing and a small hospital for the most needy. With the help of the government, the Committee formed a plan for resettling those of the black poor who would agree.[19] Although there may have been a degree of racism in this idea, many poor blacks favoured the idea, thinking they were being re-settled in the British possession of Nova Scotia, where many other black loyalist Americans had settled. The destination was not to be Novia Scotia, however, but Sierra Leone, thought to be the best place for the large number of stateless blacks. When the plot was discovered by the black poor, they were reluctant to go to Sierra Leone owing to its poor reputation as a notorious slaving area. To encourage the black poor, key black 'corporals' were used helped by some highly reputable members of the black population of London such as the educated ex-slave Olaudah Equiano. In a shameful episode, black people were eventually rounded up off the streets of London whether they wanted to go or not, some of their provisions and other aid being embezzled by the Committee's agents. The new black colonists sailed to Sierra Leone on 9th April, 1787, numbering 350 black settlers, including 41 women and 59 white wives.[20] Claims that these white women were prostitutes have since been discredited by the author Mary Beth Norton, who identified a large number of interracial families.[21] This claim may have been due to the reluctance to accept that respectable white women would choose black husbands as a matter of choice, a problem that would dog the lives of many white wives as the Liverpool Black Community matured into a mixed-race community.

These settlers on the West African Coast were known as 'Creoles', a term for people born in the Americas. Knowing and understanding only too well the white man's money and having sworn never to be enslaved again, they were to form a powerful middle-class between the European traders and the African nations of the interior. The formation of the Sierra Leone Colony was to have great implications for the black population of Liverpool, as there were often blood links between the Liverpool settlers and the new colony, both having the same loyalist roots. Sierra Leone itself was to play a large part in contributing to the growth of the Liverpool Black Community.

The Black American Loyalists were the first of a long tradition of black British colonials fighting for what they believed to be 'King and country', only to follow their white allies home to Britain - to what colonial blacks believed to be their own 'mother country', having been educated to believe precisely that. In Liverpool, we find a number of black settlers giving their birthplace as America in the parish registers of St. James,[22] in the area of black settlement. Although Liverpool was not the centre of the Black Loyalists in Britain (most being taken to London after the American Revolutionary War) since the port of Liverpool was the main Atlantic springboard to America, it is not surprising to find a number of ex-servicemen on the return journey choosing to travel no further after disembarking at Liverpool. As Liverpool was also the chief port of disembarkation from Ireland, many of the later

Irish immigrants bound for America who flooded Britain after the potato famine in the 1840s made exactly the same choice, also staying in the poorer parts of the town and maintaining the multi-racial character of the black settlement area. To this day, Liverpool Districts 8 and 1 have never constituted a black ghetto as such, the descendants of settlers from Norway, Hong Kong, other parts of Europe and the British Isles living alongside those of black settlers.

As the community historian Dorothy Kuya claims, the element of brotherhood in present-day people of the African Diaspora is by no means simply one of ideology. The names of descendants of Black Loyalist soldiers to be found in Liverpool can still be found in the United States, Canada, where the Loyalists retreated to initially, Liverpool, their first staging post in Britain and Sierra Leone, where many ended up. As many

◄ This old soldier reduced to begging is not a black Loyalist of the American War of Independence, but belongs to a later period, the 1890s. He is actually a tipster at Liverpool's Aintree Racecourse.

(by Richard Eastham, courtesy of Liverpool City Libraries)

slave owners had possessions in the West Indies, these names are also very familiar to Liverpudlians who know their ancestry to be Caribbean. Links between all possessing the same name could, of course, be those of blood or simply because of ancestors having the same owner as the Loyalists, resulting in 'slave names' as modern Americans call them.

SLAVES AND SERVANTS

Although Liverpool represented the third leg of the three-cornered Atlantic Slave Trade and slave cargoes as such did not reach the port directly from Africa, a number of black slaves, both single and as groups, were offered for sale in the town. One advertisement in the 'Williamson's Advertiser', a Liverpool newspaper in 1766 reads

"To be sold on the Exchange Coffee House in Water Street, this day the 12th September, at one o'clock precisely, Eleven Negroes imported per Angola." [23]

▲ **In this portrait of the noblewoman Catherine-Marie Legendre by J. B. Santerre, painted about 1705, the face of the small black child is almost obscured. This reflects prevailing attitudes towards black slaves and servants, who would be considered mere baubles to enhance their owner's whiteness. Note the brass collar, usually bearing the owner's name.**

(By permission of the board of Trustees of the National Museums and Galleries on Merseyside (Lady Lever Art Gallery, Port Sunlight)

Slaves, usually previously advertised in newspapers, were auctioned in the shops and coffee houses, the steps of the Custom House on the east side of the Old Liverpool Dock (now Canning Place) also being used for this purpose. On Liverpool's Exchange Flags, still in existence behind the Town Hall, the chief topics of interest were the prices of slaves, sugar and rum.[24]

There is no doubt that many early poor blacks named in the following chapter did not originally choose to live in Liverpool of their own free will. Poor blacks, at the end of the eighteenth century, by and large included slaves, ex-slaves employed as servants, and discharged sailors and soldiers from the American war. It has been mentioned that African children and young adults whose

---

LIVERPOOL BLACK LOYALIST SURNAMES

Just a few of the names of Black Loyalists still to be found in Liverpool are -

Amos	*Nelson*
Brown	*Peters*
Charles	*Smith*
Cole	*Snowball*
Ford	*Taylor*
Gorman	*Thomas*
Green	*Thompson*
Griffith	*Ward*
Johnson	*Warren*
Jones	*White*
Martin	*Williams*
Moore	*Wilson*

This list is by no means exhaustive.

▶ Exchange Flags was the scene of slaves being sold in the public houses in the eighteenth and nineteenth centuries.

prosperous parents desired such an education deemed useful for European trade would be sent to Europe, usually under the guardianship of English traders. A 17 year-old African boy, William Thomas, mentioned in the parish registers of St, James as living with a Mr. Davies in Rodney Street, still in the 1990s an upmarket partly residential street in Liverpool City Centre,[25] might well have been one of these children - rather than a servant - as during the last half of the eighteenth century there were quite a number of children with this sort of background to be found in Liverpool and the surrounding area.[26] Although the strength of racist propaganda of plantation owners and others making a living out of the Slave Trade may have later had a levelling down effect upon all black people settling in Britain, not all early black settlers were slaves, servants or the descendants of slaves, an assumption often made by some students of Liverpool Black history with the hindsight of present stereotypes of black people.

BLACK SAILORS

One of the largest single contributions to the Liverpool Black population is that of black sailors settling in the port. From the earliest days of the Slave Trade, ship's captains had been accompanied by black slaves and servants; one advertisement offering...

"For Sale immediately, ONE stout [i.e. strong] NEGRO young fellow, about 20 years of age, that has been employed for 12 months on board a ship, and is a very serviceable hand. And a NEGRO boy, about 12 years old, that has been used since Sept. last to wait at a table, and is of a very good disposition, both warranted sound. Apply to Robert Williamson, Broker."[27]

It was not long before Africans were serving on European ships as free sailors (insofar as any sailors were free in the days of the pressgang!) in their own right. The West African coast was notorious for its reputation as 'the White Man's Grave'. As some coastal peoples, such as the Kru of present day Liberia, had a tradition of seamanship, trading and fishing along considerable stretches of the West African coast, Africans were sometimes recruited to replace English sailors [28] who had died or deserted. Life could be just as hazardous for black sailors as it was for black student sons and daughters of African rulers travelling to England. There was the ever-present danger of being sold into slavery on the auction block alongside fellow Africans drawn from all stations of life, including the unfortunate children of African kings who would never see them again. Those early black sailors who did manage to survive the rigours of the journey would sometimes disembark in such ports as Liverpool, having been laid off and awaiting a return journey home or another voyage.[29] It is not unusual to find many black sailors often stayed in the port from either choice or necessity, depending on employment opportunities or the willingness of shipowners to employ blacks.

Early black sailors were usually employed as ship's cooks or stewards, many present-day black families in Liverpool owing their origins to these beginnings. Later in the nineteenth century, after the Abolition of Slavery, the Elder Dempster Shipping Line had something of a tradition of employing Africans and has indirectly played a large part in the settling of black people in Liverpool.[30] One ready source of post-Abolition immigration has, indeed, been black seamen employed on ships travelling between Liverpool and West Africa. Such shipping lines as Brocklebank had long employed black West Indians as seamen, but with the advent of steam-driven ships and the increasing colonisation of Africa, the convenience of using West African "hot seas" sailors as firemen and stokers by such lines as Elder Dempster had a two-fold advantage. One reason was the inhospitable climate of the West African coast;[31] the other reason, at least after the first decade of the twentieth century, was that Africans provided a cheap labour source.

Both white and African seamen were paid at the same rate until the seamen's strike of 1911, which resulted in a sharp differentiation in salary and exploitation. African seamen's wages were reduced from £3. 10s 0d to £2. 10s 0d per month, while white seamen's increased from £3. 10s to £5 (although some "old timers" in the Liverpool Black Community say that their own wages were not reduced in every case). Economic reasons such as this may have caused some African seamen to decide to find work on shore, along with those paid off in Liverpool to suite the needs of the shipping companies who were interested in maintaining a reserve of cheap labour in the port. The number of black settlers rose steadily between the mid nineteenth century and the outbreak of the First World War. Some shipping

▶ Liverpool Custom House steps were the scene of slave auctions in the eighteenth century.

▶ Sailors aboard their ship in Liverpool Docks c. 1900

lines, such as Elder Dempster still maintained a hostel in Liverpool for its labour reserve as late as 1925, where its seamen were retained at a fee of 12/- per week while unemployed. Most of the other companies had a series of semiofficial arrangements with boarding house-keepers - jobs being reserved for the clients of the house.[32]

THE ESTABLISHMENT OF THE BLACK COMMUNITY

One of the myths relating to the continuity of the black people in Britain is the belief by some historians that at the beginning of the nineteenth century, the black population in Britain had begun to decline and by the 1850s there were very few black people to be found in Britain at all. This is sometimes based on the popular belief that the Abolition of the Slave Trade in 1807, followed by the Abolition of Slavery itself in the Empire in 1834, ended any further reason for black people to live in Britain until the twentieth century.[33] Those historians who now question this belief now recognize both the existence of a British-born black community and the continuous exchange of people between continents, islands and the myriad of nations and races that made up the British Empire. There was undoubtedly a decline in British interest in West Africa following the Abolition of Slavery, reaching its lowest point around 1865, but the dawn of the new imperialism and the partitioning of the African continent began only a few years later, in the late 1870s.[34] During the period between the Abolition of the Slave Trade and the colonial period, there was never a time when there was not a black presence in Britain and a continuous black population in Liverpool.

It is difficult to say exactly what the size of the black community was in the eighteenth century, as only a few commentators give any precise figures. Even then, usually only particular groups are referred to, such as the numbers of black students in Liverpool in 1780 mentioned by the contemporary author Wadström,[35] but by the end of the period covered in this book the population is known to have grown to at least 3,000.[36] The Liverpool black community would appear to have been continually added to since its beginning, a factor that has perhaps tended to hide the true antiquity of the Liverpool black population as members of older families married more recent settlers, including newly arrived immigrants. Another of the confusions often encountered in establishing just how long any particular family might have lived in Liverpool is that whilst some families have lived in Liverpool continuously, some black families or individuals have left Britain only to have family members return and settle at a later point in history. In some cases, this coming and going may have taken place several times, according to the fortunes of the family. Examples of this have already been mentioned as being common amongst students returning to their countries of origin and sending their own children or even grandchildren at a later date to stay with relatives. Many black families in present-day Liverpool owe their origins in Britain to this tradition, including the Brew, Eyo and Cole families, mentioned later in detail in the following chapter. Some families have long forgotten this cycle of events and relationships with other longer established black families with a common ancestor and are often believed to be the children or grandchildren of recent immigrants with no previous connection with Britain.

In Liverpool, the fate of many earlier black students and other black visitors became irrevocably intertwined with that of the black settlers they often boarded with. Some West Indian and West African students, sailors, soldiers and workers, having come to view Britain as the "motherland" in which "the streets were paved with gold", were reluctant to return to their home countries and declare their "failure" to a family who had not the personal experience of living in an increasingly racist Britain when, finding the way blocked at every turn in the prevalent ethos of the time, life became too hard. By the end of the period of this study, the sons and daughters of former African slaves; black servants; African students, often the sons of African rulers, and, indeed, both poor English and Irish whites, along with those white women of higher station who were ostracised for their liaisons with blacks and having chosen black husbands, had become one; almost an homogeneous dual-heritage people, continually being added to, living in a restricted area that constituted a ghetto.

In Chapter Seven, "Friends and Allies", the issue of racial intermarriage will be examined more closely, but it would be true to say that from the beginning of black settlement, owing to the ratio of black male settlers to black women, the Liverpool Black Community has been a mixed-race society. The idea of black/white marriages ever being love-matches was often met with disgust by prejudiced individuals, particularly at the time of the settlement of the Black American Loyalists in Liverpool and London during the eighteenth century, when a sourly sarcastic denial appeared in a 1786 newspaper:

"When the late Mr. Dunning was some years ago reasoning against making this country a refuge for all the blacks who chose to come here, he observed "that the numerous dingy-coloured faces which crowded our streets, must have their origin in our wives being terrified when pregnant, by the numerous Africans who were to be seen in all parts of the town, and if the legislature did not take some method to prevent the introduction of any more, he would venture to prophecy, that London would, in another century, have the appearance of an Ethiopian colony.[37]

As the Liverpool Black Community became established and grew in size, this maturation into a mixed-race society caused it to become almost 'blurred at the edges' so to speak. Through intermarriage, some families or family members became increasingly light-skinned, many having the range of skin colour within a single extended family. Many of the descendants of the earliest black settlers have 'disappeared' into the rest of British society with the dilution of their black genes in much the same way as Roman, Saxon, Viking, Norman and the many Irish and later Norwegian settlers have become part of the British people. Those black British who still retain their black pigmentation have not been accepted to anything like the same degree and have remained the core of the present day black community. On the issue of dual heritage, Jackie Wilkie, of

▲ **Albert Edward James, the grandson of black settler, Edward James. 'Teddy' grew up to be a Buckingham Palace guard in the 1930s, many years before the publicity about the first black guardman in recent decades. As seen by this photograph, this clearly referred only to visibly black, as African genes are part of the makeup of the British people.**

settlers and their descendants, but that of the African gene-bank is without doubt. Visibly white notables with an African ancestor who have made their mark in European civilisation rank amongst their number the great Russian poet, Alexander Pushkin, the grandson of Peter the Great's black servant; the French author Alexander Dumas (the author of the famous action story, "The Three Musketeers"), the son of one of Napoleon's black West Indian generals and, in our own time, the talented British actor Sir Peter Ustinov, who has a great-grandmother who was Ethiopian.[38]

an old Liverpool Black family said at the time of the birth of his son -

> *"When I encounter words like half-breed, I am more aware of the person's ignorance in that respect, because I know where my blackness lies and that is in my heart, it's not the tone of my skin. If it is OK for me it will be OK for my son, unless he has a different temperament. But I will provide everything I can for him to make it easier. He won't face the obstacles that I may have faced during my life, and will face, and if he does, I will be there to help him over it."*

In social terms, the possession of a black skin remains a negative attribute in European society, but the contribution of not only visibly black

TIME SCALE

DATES	EVENTS
1699	*The Liverpool Merchant* (Captain Webster) the first legally recognised slave ship set sail from Liverpool.
1700	*The Liverpool Merchant* arrived in Barbados with 220 slaves from Africa
1730	The children of African rulers, offered a European education, begin to arrive in Britain, Liverpool particularly. Slaves are now commonly seen in Britain.
1740-	Liverpool overtook London and Bristol as the main slave trading port until the Abolition of Slavery.
1750-	Some records giving the age of Liverpool-born blacks in their maturity indicate that black people were being born in the port from around this time.
1752	A list of 101 Liverpool merchants trading in Africa included 12 who had been or who were to become mayors of Liverpool. Slave traders owned 10 of Liverpool's most prominent banks listed after 1750.
1760-	Slaves were being sold in auctions taking place in public houses and the Customs House steps in Liverpool.
1783	American Black Loyalists begin to arrive in Liverpool and London following the American War of Independence 1775-1782. Many settled in Liverpool.
1790-	Liverpool-born black children become far more common, many the offspring of Black Loyalist settlers.
1803-1815	The Napoleonic Wars brought black sailors and soldiers to Liverpool, as in all of Britain's wars. Many black sailors took part in the Battle of Trafalgar.
1807	The British Government made the Slave Trade illegal, but slavery itself continued in the West Indies.
1834	Abolition of Slavery in the British Empire.
1854-56	The Crimean War brought more settlers to Liverpool and the rest of Britain, including the famous Mary Seacole.
1870-	A new British interest in Africa begins with the New Colonial period, the 'Opening Up of Africa'. This brings mores black settlers to Liverpool as part of the 'to and fro' of Empire, as well as commerce.
1914-1918	World War I resulted in black ex-soldiers and sailors settling in Liverpool once again, typical of all of Britain's wars over a two century period.

VISITORS AND SETTLERS

Putting names and faces to the facts and figures behind the growth of the Liverpool Black Community serves to illustrate the lives of early black settlers by putting 'flesh on the bones' of historical fact. Who were those early black visitors and settlers? What were their daily lives like and why did some choose to settle in Liverpool? Are their descendants still to be found in the city?

BLACK STUDENT VISITORS
Peter Mesurado: Father and Son

The memory of some early black visitors and settlers to Liverpool has sometimes survived because of their higher social rank. An early example of the policy of seeking to indoctrinate the future kings of African kingdoms can be seen in attempts to influence successive generations of the rulers of the kingdom of Mesurado, now part of present day Liberia, through the medium of education. The friendship of the rulers of the powerful kingdom of Mesurado had long been sought by the European powers for commercial and political reasons. To the alarm of the English, the French had succeeded in winning the confidence of Mesurado, the king who offered any spot in his kingdom they chose to form a colony.[1] In the mid-eighteenth century, an opportunity presented itself to redress this balance in the British favour. The prominence of Liverpool in the African Trade predetermined it as a centre for the education of influential

Africans. Captain Peter, King of Mesurado from a succession of rulers given the same nickname by European traders and ships' captains since at least 1724, was himself educated in Liverpool and intended his son to follow his lead.[2] Unfortunately this was not to be. In the previous chapter, it is mentioned that the journey of royal African students to Europe was often fraught with danger, as once outside their own country they faced the possibility of being treated as just another black destined for the auction block. In his "Essay on Colonization" written in 1794, the author Wadström descibed how, in 1781, he himself had discovered a black child of 10 or 11 years about to embark upon a vessel bound for Sierra Leone. This dejected figure, known variously as Peter Nassau or Peter Panah turned out to be no less than the son of King Peter of Mesurado, having been kidnapped by an unscrupulous British captain and sold into slavery in the West Indies, a fate that was to bedevil many a would-be African student of Western culture. Mistreating students of this rank was obviously frowned upon by the British Government for political reasons, irrespective of how their fellow enslaved blacks were treated, and in this case there was certainly a danger to British interests. Upon arrival in the West Indies, young Peter had been recognised by another enslaved countryman as one of the King's children by a distinguishing mark on his breast. When this fact became known in Grenada to a trader of dual heritage named Johnson, he saw an opportunity for personal gain, as commercial interests in England were very much aware that the King of Mesurado would not take such poor treatment of one of his children lightly.[3] Johnson brought Peter to England, hoping for financial reward, but as this venture failed, rather than return to the West Indies to recoup the £60 paid for Peter, the dealer managed to persuade the Abolitionist Granville Sharp to grant him and his slave plots of land in the new colony of Sierra Leone, no doubt speculating that once on African soil, Captain Peter might show his gratitude more directly. Wadström succeeded in rescuing young Peter on 6th May 1788 in the presence of the Abolitionist Thomas Clarkson, paying £20 for his release.[4] He then undertook the education of Peter at his own expense, with the support of William Wilberforce and two other gentlemen. Peter was placed at a Mr. Dempster's academy at Mitcham in Surrey. Although kidnapped whilst young and well acquainted with British everyday life, he never did overcome a degree of homesickness, a factor which casts some doubts on the efforts of Wadström, which effectively prevented his return home as Johnson had intended, albeit for his own gain. In the event, this exercise, with its intention of regaining the confidence of a future African ruler, proved fruitless. One evening, two years later, Peter fell ill after sleeping on some damp grass outside Mr. Dempster's academy. This soon developed into a "a galloping consumption" which defied available treatment and the unhappy heir to Mesurado died in Wadström's own house, at the estimated age of 18-20 years. Wadström commented, in a way that at first glance seems creditworthy, reflecting the bond of affection between pupil and patron until the lack of choice on young Peter's part is remembered, that during the time that he was under his care, (2½ years) Peter had not cost more than £67. 10. 5d. He added that "though it pleased providence to call him hence", he would not regret this expenditure.[5]

James Cleveland

James Cleveland (died 1791), a powerful slave dealer, of dual heritage, was educated in Liverpool, the son of a white slaver said to be born of a "respectable Devonshire family".[6] To the annoyance of his patrons, this student put his education to his own personal use, rather than becoming a submissive pawn of white merchants involved in the African Trade. The slave trader Cleveland was said to have devastated and seriously depopulated the country south of Sierra Leone.[7] His mode of operation being to loan goods to weaker chiefs and in cases of default would attack the debtor's town with two or three hundred of his grumettas (servants). Admitted as highly intelligent by his enemies, Cleveland protected himself from counter-attack by

organising a "purrah" (sometimes known as a poro) or confederacy, by which the principal chiefs, including Cleveland, defended each other. This negative image contrasts with another opinion of Cleveland, given by an abolitionist Wadström as the wrongheaded view of a slave trader, but it certainly shows the importance of noting the origin of historical sources and the particular leanings, political and otherwise, of any particular author who may have not liked Cleveland. This slave trader speaking about Cleveland, said that he was a very gentleman-like, educated, sensible and respectable kind of man. When he was asked if Cleveland had been guilty of many excesses, the trader replied that he would make war sometimes on headmen owing him debts and would sell some of their people, if he could catch them; or perhaps carry off the inhabitants of a town, when given permission by a king or local ruler, but all in all he was a good, humane, man, for he did not shed blood if he could avoid it, and would not necessarily sell as many as he had the power to sell. [8]

Nevertheless, whilst adopting a degree of caution in judging his character and accepting that Cleveland was a man of his times, he still presents a fearsome figure. It is interesting that although operating south of Sierra Leone, in the country bordering Mesurado, Cleveland did not dare to enter the domain of that other Liverpool black student, the all too powerful King Peter! [9]

Otto Ephriam

Britain not only strengthened trading links through gaining the friendship of the children's royal fathers, but, hopefully some of the young African students, indoctrinated during their stay, might succeed to their fathers' stool (the West African version of a throne). The name of another such student who received his education in Liverpool has come down to us as one of the late eighteenth century rulers of the Efik, a people of present-day Nigeria. Calabar, the Efik country of the 'Oil Rivers' in the Niger delta, was ruled by a sophisticated hierarchy of chiefs who encouraged Europeans to build forts and factories in the area. Otto Ephraim is recorded as speaking English very well and described by at least one European as behaving and conducting himself "as politely as an English gentleman", in common with other principal men of the area. [10]

Otto's Western education was by no means voluntary, however, and appears to be totally unexpected. This Liverpool student received his European education in the most unfortunate of circumstances. In 1767, a number of British ships including the "Edgar" of Liverpool, became involved in a rivalry between the principal chiefs of Old Calabar and the residents of New Town. A number of caboceers (chiefs) of Old Town were enticed aboard, only to be imprisoned or slaughtered by the ships' crews, those that did manage to escape being annihilated by the residents of New Town lying in wait on the shore.[11] In a letter written by the former Captain of the "Edgar" in 1773, some six years after this incident, which was to become known as the "Massacre of Old Calabar", we are offered a picture of the early life of the young Ephraim, one of the imprisoned survivors:

"Liverpool, 11th November

Mr. Thos, Jones,

Sir - Yours of 7th I received wherein you desire I will send an Affadavit concerning the two black men you mention, Little Ephraim and Ancoy, in what manner the ware taken off the coast, and that I know them to be brothers of Grandy Ephraim Robin John; as to little Ephraim, I remember him very well, as to Ancoy Rob. Rob. John I cant recollect I ever saw him...I bought young Ephraim home, and had him at school near two years, then sent him out, he cost me above sixty pounds and when his fathers gone I hope the son will be a good man..."[12]

In reproducing letters written by Otto Ephraim himself, we are allowed a rare glimpse into the standard of English attained by an early black student in Liverpool, whilst providing an idea of the value of closer trading relations based on personal friendship rather than business, clearly the aim of the British in bringing chiefs' sons home. In this letter to his old patron, the trader he was boarded with, Otto seems to remember him and the family he grew up alongside with some affection and appears to have maintained links:

"Old Town Old Callabar
March 20th 1783

"Mr. Lace,

Sir,

I will take this opportunity by Captain Faireweather we have no News here of only Tom King John come down to live with my father is here now with us Orrock Robin John is dead May 24th 1783 (?) we give all his coppers to his both son George and Ephraim Orrock Send me some writing papers and 1 Bureaus to buy.

Your Humble Servant

Otto Ephraim"

P.S. Remember me to your Wife and your son Joshua Ambrose William and Polly.

Mr. Ambrose Lace
Merchant in Liverpool
Sent by ship "Jenny" [13]

As a young student in Liverpool, Otto lived in the home of his patron, Captain Ambrose Lace, in George Street, off Old Hall Street, in the town centre. Piecing together glimpses of Otto's everyday life in Liverpool from the facts available is difficult, but they do provide a picture that is not too fanciful. One of his near neighbours was a Thomas Peake, a schoolmaster and, whilst there is no evidence to suggest that he played a part in Otto's education, one wonders how a busy ship's captain would have found the time to provide tuition without help of this sort. Similarly, one can only guess at what the little African boy, still getting to grips with the English language and learning new words daily, would have made of their next door neighbour, Mr. Desaubrys, a dancing master with the frighteningly evocative Christian name (if such a name could be called Christian) of Deville![14]

THE CONTINUITY OF THE LIVERPOOL BLACK COMMUNITY

One of the characteristics of the Liverpool Black Community is that, unlike other British cities with a history of black settlement such as London and Bristol, Liverpool's black population is continuous, some families being as old as ten generations. Some families have a continuity in a different sense, in that, whilst their parents or grandparents might be recent immigrants to Britain, there is often a very long family connection, their own great grandfathers possibly even being settlers who have returned to their old homeland, only to have their children return to Liverpool.

THE EYO FAMILY

The early African student, Otto Ephraim, is a very good example of a family/clan connection between early settlers and visitors and the present-day black population of Liverpool. The children and grandchildren of King Honey Eyo, an Efik king of Nigeria, are to be found in Liverpool. King Honey settled in Liverpool at the end of the period covered in this book and is typical of a family lineage which spans several generations, involving perhaps several comings and goings between Liverpool and Africa.

The tale of the founding of the Eyo Clan is like a European fairy-tale, with all the ingredients of a bold but humble knight winning the hand of a princess. The Eyo family are descended from Eyo Nsa, a great warrior who played a large part

Old Calabar River.
There seems to be a great monopoly of the trade in this river - "Faith" went 50 miles up Calabar River and anchored off Dukestown - 4 vessels at Anchor - 3 English (Liverpool) and 1 Dutchman.
The "Abeona" of Liverpool was just commencing trade with the natives - went on board and found "King Eyo Honesty" and 3 or 400 natives with him receiving the "Dash" - his Majesty shook hands all round, asked a few questions and drank champagne.

◀ A letter written by the captain of a Liverpool ship, the "Faith", describing a face to face meeting with King Eyo Honesty, the founder of the Eyo clan of South-East Nigeria. By permission of James E. Cowden and John O. C. Duffy, authors of "The Elder Dempster Fleet History 1852-1985" and publishers Mallet and Bell.

►Ephraim Town, Old Calabar, showing King Eyo Honesty's canoe being saluted by the guns of Her Majesty's sloop "Rattler". (Based on a drawing in the possession of Dr. K. Onwuka Dike, University College, Ibadan).

in the war between Creektown and Old Calabar in 1767. He is also remembered as a national hero who defeated the powerful Mbiakong pirates who constantly attacked Efik trade-canoes. Although he was originally a slave, the local king (one of the six Efik kings), Esien Ekpe Oku, gave him his daughter in marriage as well as his freedom. Eyo Nsa, known to European traders as King Willy Honesty, or King Eyo Honesty, grew rich and formed his own 'ward' or domain, founding the Eyo Clan, as well as inheriting an important priesthood role after his father in law's death. Eyo Honesty is not related to Otto Ephraim himself, being on the opposite side to Otto's older brother, King Ephraim Robin John, in the Efik civil war, but his children were related, as were all the kings of the Efik; descended from a common ancestor. All his descendants, therefore, are related through his wife to Otto Ephraim. In 1805, Eyo Nsa (or 'Eyo Honesty'), described as "King of Ebongo" (mistakenly, as this is the name of his priesthood. the "Ebunko") was said to be about six feet high with an extremely good-natured countenance and a very commanding deportment. Once again, the fact that he was a great warrior was mentioned. [15]

What the story of Eyo Nsa does tell us is that the concept of African Slavery was very different from that of European slavery. In African slavery, a slave might not only inherit, but, as in this case,

might actually become a ruler in his own right, his decendants passing automatically into the ranks of the nobility. A comparison with Caribbean and American slavery paints an entirely different picture, a history of perpetual servitude that still remains as a residue of the legacy of the Slave Trade.

THE BREW FAMILY: AN AFRICAN POCAHONTAS

The importance of Liverpool's role in the education of those black people who had come to be part of its very life-blood cannot be underrated. The prominence of Liverpool facilitated the growth of a settled black community drawn from demobbed black soldiers and sailors after the War of American Independence and Britain's later wars, servants and freed slaves of the then townships' inhabitants, and those black students who chose not to return to their countries of origin, something of a tradition that has continued to the present day.

The Liverpool Black Community has many families who owe their origins to the above tradition. The dual heritage descendants of a trader on the West African Coast, Richard Brew (1725-76) [16] are now to be found in Liverpool. The great

A LIVERPOOL PRINCESS

▲ Schoolgirl Adain Iniabere, a descendant of King John Bannashee Corrantee of Anomabu, Ghana, through her great-grandfather, the Liverpool settler Henry Brew, may not be considered a princess in modern Liverpool, but she certainly is by the author!

▲A portrait of William Ansah in *Gentleman's Magazine* Vol XX (1751), 29 years after his visit to England.

become a contradiction in terms owing to the growth of racialism. The contrast between the experience of an ancestral relative of Henry's, William Ansah, brother of Richard's wife, and that of Henry himself (this family being yet another example of successive waves of the same family visiting or settling in Britain), is noteworthy. Being of a noble African family, William, the son of John Bannishee Corrantee, the Ohinnee (ruler) of Anomabu, had been treated well upon his arrival in England in the 1730s, if the fact that he, like young Peter Mesurado, was sold into slavery by a rogue captain and later rescued, is ignored! William, feted by society, was not only applauded by an audience of the opera in Covent Garden, but was introduced to King George in one occasion.[17] (the fact that his portrait was found in 'Gentleman's Magazine, Volume XX' says everything!) Two hundred years later, Henry, on

grandfather of Spencer Brew, a student at Hope University College in present day Liverpool, was Henry Brew, a descendant of another Henry, the son of Richard Brew, a one-time Governor of Anomabu Coastal Fort, now in modern Ghana, and an African wife, the daughter of a local king. Believed to have been Manx or Irish, Richard was a colourful figure who played a prominent part in coastal trade and the early hostilities between Britain and her Fante allies against the powerful Ashanti Empire. As part of West African coastal society, Richard's Fante descendants rated Western education highly. Spencer's great grandfather arrived in England in the 1920s to further his education, which he hoped to complete in America. In the event, having found a wife en route (the daughter of the Bermudian Edward James) and settled in Liverpool in the 1930s, Henry became a merchant seaman, not an unfamiliar occupation for West African Coastal peoples settled in British ports.

What is interesting in this particular instance is that it affords the opportunity to observe the changes that had taken place in how black people were perceived in Britain by the early twentieth century compared with the eighteenth century. By this time, the idea of a black gentleman had

▼ Henry Brew with a white in-law

◄ George Butler of Ghana, during a visit to his Brew cousins. Left to right are George Butler, Harriet Brew, Joan Brew, baby Kenneth and a friend.

the other hand, faced hostility, not only in his social life, owing to prevalent social attitudes to black people during the1930s, but he also suffered a good deal of difficulty in finding employment, both on land and sea. Both these students, though separated by generations, were members of the same family, it should be remembered, and of the same social standing back in the then Gold Coast, now modern Ghana. The origin of this family is even more like the story of Pocohantas and John Smith than the fairytale origins of the Eyo family in that the founder, Richard Brew, like Smith, was white. In both cases, truth is more interesting than fiction!

King John Corrantee was pro-British, but took the precaution of sending another son to France to keep each European nation on its toes! When William was enslaved John insisted that the British should help him and sent yet another son, Frederick, to accompany him to England[18]. This family later sent yet another member to England, this time to Liverpool, providing one of the Liverpool connections to the present Brew family. When Africans became Christians, they often took European names. St James Parish Registers record, "George Butler. Native of Annomaboe in Africa.w.b. April 3rd 1785" (w.b. meaning 'was baptised')[19]. George returned to Anamabo and the Brew family are aware of the fact that not only are the Butler family of Ghana known to be cousins, descended from a commonancestor, but there are more than one 'George Butlers' still visiting their cousins in Liverpool from Africa today. Name combinations in that family today include George Butler, George Brew Butler and George Brew.

▼ Samuel Cole, taken before the Great War.

▲ Benjamin Nowell-Ross is a great-grandson of Samuel Cole.

Leone in the late eighteenth century. It is possible that, like William Henry Pratt, the ancestor of the Sierra Leonean Pratt family, also in present-day Liverpool, he was rescued from slavery a few years later than the American Black Loyalists. What is certain is that Christian Frederick Cole was the grandson of this first Cole, Thomas, who was an Ibo of present-day Nigeria who had been captured like his fellow Ibo, William Pratt. Christian is attributed with being the first African graduate at Oxford in 1876,[20] though the distinction of being the first black person was to go to Alexander Heslop, a West Indian who graduated from Queen's College Oxford, as early as 1835.[21] Over the past two centuries, many members of the Cole family have visited and settled in Liverpool, there being now at least four black families of that name in Liverpool; all aware of their Sierra Leone ancestry if not the relationship between their families.

▼ Jim Clarke sparring with two friends. One is thought to be the Olympic swimmer Austin Rawlinson.

THE COLE FAMILY

Samuel Cole was a seaman from Sierra Leone who settled in Liverpool during the First World War. He has many descendants living in the port with various surnames, obviously according to the marriages of his daughters. A few of the family names now descended from Samuel living in Liverpool include Kadiri, Nowell, Thomas and Morris. Born in 1884, Samuel served in the Merchant Navy as a 'donkeyman', one of the most dangerous jobs, as the engine rooms were a prime target for enemy u-boats. He also worked for several shipping firms.

The first Cole in Sierra Leone was a freed slave who may have been a black American Loyalist soldier, who, having passed through Britain after the American Colonies were lost to Britain, was re-settled like many other freed slaves in Sierra

THE CLARK FAMILY

James Clarke is distinguished by being the only black man in Liverpool to have a street called after him. Vincent Clarke, his son, recalls that as a boy, Jim did not live in the area of black settlement, but in the north end of the City, where he is still remembered with affection by those who knew him in what was almost exclusively a poor white district. Born in Jamaica in 1880, he stowed away in a ship bound for Liverpool when he was only 14 years old and was adopted by a family of Irish descent in St. Augustines parish church in the Scotland Road district of Liverpool.

Jim's great gift was swimming and he was respected by everyone for his skill. As an adult he lived in Elizabeth Terrace in the parish of St. Sylvesters, where he taught many of the local children to swim. A member of the Everton Swimming Club, which had won the North Lancashire League Cup several times, Jim often saved people from drowning in the deep canal nearby which ran between Burlington Street and Athol Street. In spite of telling their children to stay away from the water many were often tempted to fish or swim in the canal in warm weather. Many children would get out of their depth and would start screaming and waving their arms around as the water filled their lungs. Ocassionally, drunks would fall into the canal on their way home. Some died, but others were lucky. If Jim was around, he would dive into the water and swim at an amazing speed towards the person who had fallen in, usually underneath the beneath the surface like a dark shadow. When the Angel of Death came for a child, Jim usually got there first.

Vincent says of his father,

"My father was a docker in the North end of Liverpool. He was a big man, six feet plus and 12 stone and was built for the sports he loved. All the local kids of our

▲ Jim Clarke was recognised as a local hero by having a street in Liverpool named after him.

32

▲ Jim Clarke's grandaughter, Beverley, with her children, Tommy, James and Stephen.

street used to wait for him to come home from work with pockets of peanuts for them, which they used to take home and roast on a shovel over the fire. After saving about 9 or 10 children from the canal, he decided to do something about it. He started going along to the local swimming baths, Burroughs Gardens in Burlington Street. The local schools took their children there and he taught a lot of them how to swim. He used to do exhibitions during galas and he enjoyed making the kids laugh by sitting on the bottom of the baths with a bucket on his head singing songs like 'Oh My Darling Clementine' and 'Jerusalem'. He also drank lemonade under water with the bucket on his head.

One of his favourite routines was a swimming act he called "Me and my shadow" with one of his friends from Everton Swimming Club. As he was a great underwater swimmer, he would swim

▼ Boys bathing in the Leeds-Liverpool Canal, Burlington Street Bridge. Taken at the end of the 19th century by Charles Frederick Inston (Courtesy of Liverpool City Libraries)

underneath, while his friend swam on top. They would turn and dive in perfect harmony, copying each other exactly to the sound of 'ooh!' and 'aah!' from the crowd. He also enjoyed making the crowd laugh by pretending to be a porpoise!

He started his swimming career at the Wavertree Swimming Club, where he won a lot of medals between 1908 and 1910, but he also swam for Bootle, Waterloo and Everton Swimming Clubs. For Everton, he won the Lancashire League Cup on many occasions. My father used to take me to the local swimming baths - when I was about five or six - where he used to carry me on his back up and down the length of the pool. I can remember screaming, because I was frightened of the water and to this day, I can't swim!

"The worse thing was when anyone fell in the canal and drowned. If they could not find the body, the police used to come around to our house, or where my father worked, and asked him to go into the water and see if he could find it. They didn't like to use the grappling irons because they tore the body to bits. The canal was the Liverpool-Leeds Canal and most of the children used to swim and play there in the hot waters behind Tate and Lyle, the sugar factory in Burlington Street. My father always had a sixth sense or a feeling where they were and he could stay under the water a long time and nearly always found the body.

My father loved swimming, running and boxing. His heroes were Jesse Owens and Jack Johnson, the World Heavyweight Boxing champion. When Jack Johnson came over to Liverpool, my father asked if he could spar for him, but he wouldn't let him. Another great favourite of his was the singer Paul Robeson. Being such a big man, he loved his food - scouse, roast potatoes and salt fish.

My father died just after the war. It started when I was three years old. He had me when he was quite old - I was the youngest. I remember the sirens, the bombs falling and the 'all clear'. They had air raid shelters in the middle of the street and I used to get carried there and put on the top bunker. I remember the tram cars and the brass bands playing in the park. I also remember the ferries and going over to New Brighton with the family. I had a mate at school - his name was John White and his mother used to tell me that my father had saved her life."

When my father died, the school children of St. Anthony and St. Sylvester's school lined the streets from our house to the church. People used to tell me that the Chief Constable of Liverpool was one of the pall-bearers, but my older brother told me he wasn't. They must have meant Austin Rawlinson, the great Olympic Champion, came to the funeral and paid his respects to my mother and family. I believe he was a policeman of high authority, but I'm not sure."

The local swimming baths just around the corner in Speke where Vincent lives is called The Austin Rawlinson Sports Centre after Jim's great friend. Austin Rawlinson did, in fact, become Assistant Chief Constable.

Forty years after his death, the Vauxhall community where Jim lived underwent many changes; new streets being built to replace the old terraced housing. The community fought for and got a street named after him. When the local community put their request to the City Council, at least three councillors knew of him already. One of these was John White, whose mother had been rescued, as she told Vincent herself, when she was a little girl of three. The motion was passed. James Clarke Street runs between Tatlock Street and Hornby Street, a fitting honour for a local hero. The local people also wanted a plaque placed on the bridge where he saved so many lives.

Liverpool, like many other cities has many such little-known local heroes, but while they are remembered with pride by their friends and family, their memory will live on for ever. In this case, all those that had cause to remember Jim Clarke happened to be white.

Jim Clarke has many descendants living in present day Liverpool, including another youthful James Clarke. Jim had begun his life as a little boy a long way away on the island of Jamaica and had ended up a local hero with a street named after him in an English City.

LATER BLACK VISITORS

The British and Foreign Anti-Slavery Society, founded in 1839 by the Quaker radical Joseph Sturge, used public indignation in support of the victims of colonial policies, often self-designated, as in the case of escaped American slaves wishing to make known the plight of their fellows by travelling around Britain giving talks. Following the lead of their meeting place and main forum in England, Exeter Hall, run by the British and Foreign Anti-Slavery, smaller "Exeter Halls" sprung up all over the country.[22] Of these halls, built by socialists in the 1840s, Liverpool possessed the largest, standing in Lord Nelson Street, near the main area of black settlement. Many black lecturers visiting Liverpool were thus offered the opportunity to provide educational programmes illustrating everyday slave life panoramas, often spiced by accounts of slave escapes.[23] One of the most well-known of these to pass through Liverpool was William Wells Brown, a black American, slavery remaining in that country until 1865. Arriving in Europe in 1849, Wells spent five years in Britain during which he spoke at 1,000 meetings to plead the cause of black people still held in bondage in the United States.

Wells was just one of a number of black visitors to Liverpool in the late nineteenth and early twentieth centuries. Marcus Garvey and other

wealthier members of the black dispora outside Africa, including the American actor Paul Robeson, both found their way to Liverpool to meet the settled black community. Almost all, if not all, of the future leaders of the formerly British independent black states in both Africa and the Caribbean that were to emerge during the 1950s were educated in Britain, seeking common cause, including such personalities as Kwame Nkrumah of Ghana, Jomo Kenyatta of Kenya, Hastings Banda of Malawi and Eric Williams of Trinidad and Tobago. Almost all of these notables who have made an impact upon world events, in turn, spent some time living in Liverpool, adding to the list of those other, British-born, black people who have made their mark upon Britain; a multicultural and multiracial society.

CHAPTER THREE

EARLY LIVERPOOL-BORN BLACK PEOPLE

Black people were being born in Liverpool by at least the latter part of the eighteenth century. Giving an address called "Old Dock", now Canning Place, in the dockland area around Liverpool's first dock, George, son of Mercurius Stevens, from Antigua, was baptised on August 6th 1795 in St. James Church, along with Thomas, the son of Jack Brown, described as 'a native of Savannah'. Another black American, Charles Williams, is baptised at the same time as his wife, Margaret, and son, Charles, on September 21st, 1997.[1] Black loyalists were shipped out of America to Britain in the late 1780s from the American port of Savannah after the British surrender to the American rebels. Both Williams and Brown are common names amongst the black loyalists, suggesting that they may have belonged to slave owners of that name.

Black children born in Liverpool were not only those of black loyalists. Some African students of royal descent have been shown in this book to have either stayed or had their descendants return at a later date, but in St. Nicholas Parish 1796, there is an intriguing entry: "Samuel Baron, son of the African king <u>Onramby</u>, alias <u>Johnson</u>, was baptised January 21st."[2] Was this prince born during a visit, or was his father a king in exile, perhaps? There are more than one Liverpool Black families named Johnson, but a little research by another student of the Liverpool

Black Community is required. Nevertheless, Samuel still qualifies as a Liverpool born black child!

THE BROWN FAMILY

Another descendant of a black American loyalist to establish a Liverpool-born black family was originally known as Cato or James Cato, after the current fashion of giving slaves classical Roman or Greek names. After living in Nova Scotia, like many black loyalists, he ran away to sea as a child and actually served on ships involved in the Slave Trade. Later, he joined the Royal Navy and changed his name to James Brown. There is a Liberian family named Brown, the anglicised name also suggesting black American ancestry, but the link between that family and the descendants of James Brown would require further research. If they are related, it would be yet another black family returning to live in Liverpool at different times in its history.

It would be difficult to find a more famous ship for James to serve upon, for James was chief boatswain on Nelson's flagship 'Victory' at the time of the battle of Trafalgar in 1804 (Liverpool's Walker Art Gallery has a painting of 'The Death of Nelson', which shows a black sailor who could well be James Brown). James was of mixed-parentage, his mother said to be a member of the prominent Liverpool merchant Gough family, another example of the fact that not all black/white marriages or liaisons were restricted to women of lower station, in spite of prejudice shown towards black people. It has been suggested that James may not be a black loyalist, but a very early Liverpool born black merely living in Nova Scotia, his birth being estimated as being around 1750. A very large man (some 20 stone in weight), when he left the Navy, James worked in Liverpool as a foundry worker, marrying three times to local women.

James had two sons; John Gough Brown, born in Liverpool in the early years of the nineteenth century, and James Brown junior (1815-1881). The older son, John, was a temperance advocate

The Early History of Britain's Oldest Black Community

36

preaching at a church in Everton Road, whilst James achieved some distinction in later life in the Isle of Man. After serving as an apprentice to a Liverpool printer in Princes Street and working for the 'Liverpool Mercury', James Brown ran the Concert Tavern, a public house off Fox Street. It was after his marriage to Eleanor, the daughter of a Scottish master mason living in the Isle of Man, that James returned to his printers' trade, working for two employers in succession who were involved in the Chartist Movement. As in the case of William Davidson, mentioned later, James became involved in the Chartist cause, writing and publishing articles championing democratic rights and eventually founding his own newspaper, the 'Isle of Man Times'. At this time, the House of Keys, the lower house of the Manx parliament, was an unelected self perpetuating oligarchy left to its own devices by the UK parliament. This drew the attention of many Manx radicals, including the adopted Manxman, the Liverpool-born James Brown. In 1863, James wrote an article that particularly offended the Keys, leading to his imprisonment in Castle Rushen.

Fortunately, by this time, James was blessed with two very able sons, the eldest of whom was able to secure his release. John Archibald was born in 1840 and eventually inherited his father's newpaper business. At the time of his father's imprisonment, John Archibald, at the age of 24, appealed to the British parliament and was able to secure James' release amidst popular demonstrations in his favour. The incident had two outcomes; James successfully sued twenty House of Keys members for £520 and costs and, more significantly, the climate created by the publicity surrounding the case of what local Manxmen nicknamed 'Darkie Brown' (apparently with some affection) led to reform of the House of Keys only three years later, the Manx lower house now becoming a democratically elected body. James' younger son, James William Ross Brown, born 1858, began his working-life with his father and brother in the printing trade, but later studied law. A lawyer at 30, James William Ross rose to the position of deputy judge, and although a prominent member of the national Liberal club, refused to stand for parliament when

◀Could the black sailor in this painting of The Death of Nelson by Daniel Maclise (1806-1870) possibly be James Brown?
The chances are he may not be, as it is estimated that as many as twenty five per cent of sailors engaged in the Battle of Trafalgar may have been black. (By permission of the Board of Trustees of the National Museums and Galleries on Merseyside (Walker Art Gallery, Liverpool)

asked. James William Ross Brown is notable in that although there were other black law students studying in Britain in the 1880s (Christian Cole, for example), most 'colonial' lawyers returned home to practise in their own countries. James William Ross differed in that he was the son of a Liverpool-born black, knowing no other country but Britain. He was not only the first person of Liverpool black ancestry to 'take the silk', but the first Manxman, practising both on the Northern Circuit and London.[3]

Censuses taken in the nineteenth century do not mention the age of either 'alien' or British-born residents,[4] but a strong hint of the antiquity of the settled black community is to be found in scattered references. In Foreign Office correspondence dealing with black people imprisoned in the United States between the years 1823 and 1851, a Henry Steward, a black sailor, gave his birthplace as Liverpool. The fact of his maturity in 1830, the year of his imprisonment, may serve as a fair indication of the age of the indigenous black community, for this was not an isolated example. A William Houston, also imprisoned in America in 1851 with a view to being sold into slavery, was, although actually born in Gibraltar, reared in Liverpool by his mother, who was of African descent.[5]

▲ James Brown whilst imprisoned in Castle Rushen. (Reproduced by kind permission of Manx National Heritage Museum)

LIVERPOOL AS A FOCUS FOR BRITISH-BORN BLACK PEOPLE

During the eighteenth and nineteenth centuries, the numbers of settlers and Liverpool-born living in Liverpool were increased by British-born black people from other parts of the country. Eric Lynch, born in Liverpool in 1932, had a British-born mother from elsewhere in the country, born in the nineteenth century.

"My mother was a British-born woman born in a place called Shotley outside Newcastle whose father had come on a sailing ship in the late 1800s. My father was a Barbadian sailor who came in the early twentieth century. In Barbados, I've traced the name Lynch to an Irish slave owner from Cork. My ancestors were from the Tate Plantation. I've researched it all and I'm off to Barbados soon to see it!"

Up until the 1980s, Liverpool had the famous Tate and Lyle Sugar Refinery, owned by the descendants of the Tate family and the equally well-known slave-owning Lyle family. Liverpool now has the Tate Art Gallery, the northern counterpart of the London based tourist attraction, built on the proceeds of the Slave Trade and the industry based on slavery.

Eric also touches upon important issues of nationality faced by Liverpool Black people and the climate they live in. The everlasting lack of recognition and constant mis-identification; the latest label being "asylum seekers" is evident in Eric's comment:

> "In my life, I've been a builders' labourer, later a trading officer, and now I'm a tourist guide, educating the public on the Slave Trade. When I first began, I was told, "I've heard such glowing reports about these guided walks you do. If you would like to give me your passport, I'll do what I can to get you a permanent job." I pointed out that I was not aware that I needed a passport!

> I was born in Newington, a street off Renshaw Street. When I was new-born a nurse commented, "Ooh, look. Another little nigger!".

There is more than one family in Liverpool named Freeman, but that of Brenda (known to her friends as 'B') Freeman dates back to an example of a British-born black ancestor from that other slave-port, Bristol:

> "My grandmother was Eva Johnson (Johnson by marriage). She was born in Bristol in 1881. Her father was a West African and her mother was white. Now, grandmother married twice and her second husband was an American Indian. Now, how come she married an American Indian? - he was a real American Indian! Well! He was known as Indian Joe and she met him in the circus - in Vaudeville. At the time, the only work that a lot of black people could get here and up and down the country was in Vaudeville, singing and dancing, and that seems to be a lot of the black British that were born in the 1800s. I haven't traced it back to whether he was in Buffalo Bill's Circus or not (Buffalo Bill visited Liverpool in the late 1800s), but my mother had always been involved in Vaudeville, theatre and pantomime, and not only her, because that was the only work they could get. If you go back to some of the biggest shows that ever came here to England - my grandmother and others - they used to tour

Background image: The old black settlement area of Liverpool provided a ready source of actors and extras for film and theatre. It is ironic that using black British in the parts of 'natives' was very useful, as they presented no language or cultural difficulties, yet they were not offered roles as 'ordinary' British citizens in films.

▲ Edward Tagoe has many descendants in various parts of Liverpool

that when black people were in theatre and travelling through towns, they weren't always able to board anywhere, there were a lot of people who used to board at my grandmother's house.

My grandmother appeared in the film, "Sanders of the River" with Paul Robeson. It was made down in Shepperton Studios and in that 'African' scene, where Paul Robeson is in the village with Sanders, who is 'the master', there were a lot of black people, all from Liverpool! There were a lot of black people at the time working out of the old film studios, so when those shows used to come over from America, like Showboat, nearly all the caste came from here in Britain for those big shows. When they were recruiting anybody, the only work that black people could get was in the theatre and Vaudeville. If you go through the history of many black families, they would have a member who worked in the theatre.

My mother herself was born in Birmingham, so it is as though some black families like ours have slowly gravitated to Liverpool, as an old settlement.

all over the country and they used to do all the theatres. Auntie Brenda, Auntie Cassie, Auntie Dora, my mother and Auntie Josie; they all used to tour with all the shows. We used to have a big double-fronted house in Berkley Street on the corner, No 1. It was blitzed during the War, but we lived next door but one to a relative of the Lewis's, another old family - that was grandma's house. It was on three floors and my grandmother lived in the basement, so there was a lot of coming and going in our house, especially people in show business, because we used to have a xylophone on the middle landing underneath the window. As kids, every time we used to run up and down the stairs, somebody was always clonking it! I believe that it was left there by somebody, because, as people used to travel through, you have got to remember

Brenda refers to an ancestor from West Africa named Johnson. Whether this is a descendant of the African king Onramby who changed his name to Johnson in Liverpool mentioned above would be an interesting piece of research.

The show-business connection is also present in other old Liverpool Black families, such as the Littles, the Maikers and the Tagoes. Eddie Tagoe is a well-known face on British television as an actor. Like Brenda's mother, who was recruited from the old Liverpool Black Community, as an obvious source for film-makers requiring black casting, one of Eddie's roles was a support member of the famous film, 'Zulu'.

The first Liverpool Tagoe, Edward, was born

in Ghana (then called the Gold Coast) in 1890. Edward was a merchant seaman who settled and married in Liverpool at the beginning of the twentieth century. He appears to have changed his name from Adu or Ado to Tagoe, name-changing being quite common amongst seamen for a number of reasons, such as age and the prejudices of families and tribes of the interior against their kin going to sea, which many thought was an occupation for sea-going coastal peoples such as the Kru. There is another explanation why Edward may have changed his name. Henry Brew, another Ghanaian, also had an additional clan name of Otu, and often used it when in the company of countrymen, but this is more common when the alternative name to the traditional family name is European (Henry had a Manx or Irish ancestor).

Edward is described by his son Norman as being quite a religious man, who died in his prime, at the age of 52, when Norman was only 14.

Another example of a British-born black person from elsewhere settling in Liverpool is Anne Jones, the eldest daughter of a Welsh woman and a Welsh-speaking slave named John Ystumllyn. John, nicknamed 'Black Jack' was kidnapped on the West African coast when he was 8 years old around 1745 and brought to Caernarvonshire. His wife was a maid-servant named Margaret and they were married in Dolgellau church in 1768. John later changed his name to Jones after being appointed steward of a local big house in the Criccieth area. Although mixed-marriages in Liverpool were usually between black men and white women, because of the scarcity of black women, occasionally white men would find black wives. Anne, John's mixed-race daughter, married a Liverpool musician and musical instrument vendor,[6] but her brother, Richard, became a huntsman in Wales for Lord Newborough. Richard died in 1862 at the age of 92 at Llandwrong, near Caernarvon. John still has descendants in the Caernarvon area, and in the 1980s a Welsh lecturer at Liverpool University,

visibly white, claimed descent from what he believed to be this line.

WILLIAM DAVIDSON: A BLACK 'GUY FAWKES'

The white male half of a mixed-marriage was far more likely to be found in the West Indies, where black female slaves had little or no choice of opinion in unions of any sort. Although not born in Liverpool, William Davidson is an example of this and his life provides an interesting picture of the politics of the nineteenth century. William Davidson's white father was the Attorney General of Jamaica, whilst his mother was a black slave. Born in 1786, William seems to have been well provided for, receiving an education in Jamaica until he was 14, then sent to finish his education in Edinburgh. He lived for three years in Liverpool as an apprentice to a lawyer, but appears to have given up his studies to run away to sea. William may have been influenced by the radical movement whilst in Edinburgh, but his experience in Liverpool seems to have provided the catalyst in causing him to re-think his life. He did resume his studies in mathematics for a time, this time in Aberdeen, but seems to have faced a number of social problems relating to his race in other parts of the country during his life.[7]

William's association with the radicals was to prove fatal. Since the French Revolution of 1789, the English ruling classes had harboured a suspicion, and fear, of their own lower orders. The growing radical movement, arising out of the need to address domestic poverty, was thought to be connected to the Abolitionist movement, often by the movements themselves, which recognised a common cause and a common enemy; the vested interests of the wealthy few.[8] Following the end of the Napoleonic War, the plight of the poor in many growing cities was made even worse by returning soldiers. In 1919, a crowd gathering to protest at their lot at Peters Field near Manchester was dispersed with particular ferocity by cavalry. William, by this time a follower of Thomas Paine, joined the Marylebone Union Reading Society in London, set up in response to what was being called the 'Peterloo Massacre'. Many radicals began openly drilling like soldiers, determined that, if a 'Peterloo' should ever happen again, they would be prepared to resist, by force, if necessary. This alarmed governmental circles even more, as the previous three decades since the French Revolution had been a tense era owing to the ever-present fear of the poor in this country following the lead of the French in insurrection.[9]

Signs of unrest reached a fever-pitch by 1819, when William became involved in a plot to kill the Cabinet whilst they sat at dinner at the Grosvenor Square house of Lord Harrowby, Lord President of the Council. The idea was for this act to be a signal for a popular uprising all over the country, but the plan was doomed to failure owing to the fact that one of the plotters' number was a police informer and an agent of the government. George Edwards acted as an agent provocateur, urging on William and his white comrades, including Arthur Thistlewood, James Ings, John Brunt and Richard Tidd, to acts of violence; no doubt in the knowledge that overt expressions of treason could be more easily stamped on by the state. This plot, called 'the Cato Street conspiracy', a loft in that street off the Edgeware Road being the place where a variety of weapons were stored, met an abrupt end with a raid by government men-at-arms. William was captured, but not before he had tried to strike the leader of the raiding party, a Lieutenant Frederick Fitzclarence, no less than the illegitimate son of the future King of England, William IV, with a cutlass.[10]

On 1 May, 1820, William Davidson and his four friends were first hanged, then, to the dismay of the sympathetic crowd, the executioner cut off each of their heads and showed them to the crowd, denouncing them as traitors. Public executions were still common and considered popular entertainment at this time, but the horror of this occasion seems to have had an impact, as this was to be the last public decapitation in Britain.[11]

Short-lived insurrections broke out in Barnsley, Huddersfield and Sheffield, but the London rising never did take place. As in the case of the Cato Street conspiracy, once again government agents in Scotland fomented strikes in Paisley and Glasgow in order to flush out would-be dissidents. The ease with which the threat of violent insurrection was dealt with at this time showed that any future efforts to meet the needs of the lower orders of British society would have to be peaceful. Finding solutions to the desperate plight of the urban and rural poor was an issue that was to occupy both black and white reformers for the remainder of the nineteenth century.[12]

GEORGE WILLIAM CHRISTIAN

Chapter One mentioned the myth that following the Abolition of Slavery in 1834, the black population in Britain declined dramatically.[13] Examples refuting the belief of some historians that by the 1850s there were no black people to be found in Britain are not difficult to find in Victorian Liverpool. George William Christian was the son of an Antiguan father and a white Liverpudlian mother. George, one of five children, was born in 69 Beaufort Street in Toxteth in 1872, later moving to 14 Robertson Street. Jacob Christian, his father, was a seaman who had left the West Indies to settle in Liverpool at the age of fifteen. His decision to become a timber merchant may have first brought him into contact with the wealthy firm of John Holt. It has been mentioned that the Holt shipping line had something of a tradition of employing black seamen and it may have been this that prompted Jacob to place George and his brother Arthur with this successful firm. George William left England for Africa at the age of fifteen to serve as a clerk for Holt. He appears to have been exceptionally gifted and soon established his own merchant trading business in Nigeria and Cameroon, eventually employing European as well as black employees.

George kept in contact with his Liverpudlian relatives and in 1911 married Isabella Stanbury, a white nurse who had nursed him back to health after an illness in Hope Street Hospital, at St. Luke's Church, Liverpool (he was apparently living in Aigburth at the time). It has been mentioned that white women marrying black husbands in Liverpool covered the whole range of social classes, including white women of higher station who were ostracised for their having chosen black husbands. Isabella was of a well-to-do family in Wallasey, the daughter of a builder and estate agent, and is an example of women who might well have been spurned by society, had it not been for the fact that she had married such a successful black husband, the loyalty of her family and that she had joined George in Africa for a large part of her life, rather than stay in England. Many white wives were less fortunate and faced lives almost as hard as their husbands in terms of social acceptance.

One of the chief difficulties Liverpool Blacks face in present-day British society is recognition of who and what they are, in terms of nationality - their distinct identity as an integral part of British society - as opposed to being seen as perpetual

▲ Edward James and his wife, Harriet Gates. (taken in the 1870s)

▼ George Christian and his wife and driver in Nigeria (Onitsha) in 1919. Reproduced from a photograph in the possession of family member Margaret Othick with the help of historian Jeffrey Green.

'immigrants'. George had a similar problem in Cameroons. The German authorities tried to treat him as a 'native' and fined and eventually expelled him for not registering a title to land. George managed to enlist the support of the M.P. for Toxteth, who had the Foreign Office appeal to Berlin, complaining that although George was, indeed, 'a mulatto' (sic), he was a British subject and should not be treated as one of their own colonial subjects.

The writer Alfred F. Calvert described George William Christian in his book,'Nigeria and its Tin Fields' (published in 1910 in London) as a pioneer trader and stressed that the success of his firm was entirely due to his exceptional qualifications. It is interesting that Calvert made no reference to the fact that George was not white. Whether this was because he did not genuinely feel it was important or because he simply did not know how to explain or justify the object of

▼ **Three of Edward James' eight children, Edith, Albert and baby Agnes.**

his admiration to a readership that might have had difficulties accepting the truth at this time, is open to conjecture.

George bought a house for his Aunt Alice and her children, and his own visits home, in Penkett Road, Wallasey in the Wirral, called 'Onitsha', after the Nigerian palm trading centre where he had a business. George died in 1924 in Cameroon.[14]

THE JAMES FAMILY

In spite of any prejudice shown towards mixed marriages during the nineteenth century, there is no doubt that many were love matches, however much other sections of the public may have disapproved. One such marriage was that of Harriet Gates and Edward James in 1873.[15] Harriet was the daughter of a Cheshire flatman who had settled in the growing town in 1853.[16] Edward was a Bermudan seaman whose steady salary provided the necessary capital for financing a succession of small confectionery businesses in the area, his wife running the shops during his long voyages. Incomes from both these sources enabled his family of eight children to keep above the bare subsistence level of many of the surrounding population, several of Edward's children attending St. Cleopas Board School, Mill Street.[17]

The James family of Liverpool present an interesting case study of a Black family of many generations who not only absorbed members from different waves of Black immigration hut also white settlers - themselves drawn to Liverpool from different parts of Britain by the opportunities created by the march of the industrial revolution and the growth of the port.

As a very young boy Edward James, like so many other Black settlers, was drawn by the traditional call of "Queen and Country" at the outbreak of the Crimean War, like the great Jamaican nurse, Mary Seacole, sometimes called 'the black Florence Nightingale.' Even at the time

▲   In this painting of John Archer by the talented Liverpool Black artist Paul Clarkson, elements of his life are cleverly encoded in the artifacts included. This fine work of art now hangs with those of past Liverpool Lord Mayors in Liverpool Town Hall.

of Edward's arrival the districts which are now Liverpool 1 and 8, closely situated to the docks as they were, were mixed-race areas. At the time the Toxteth area was still inhabited by wealthy merchants and it was into this mixed-race area that Edward James settled.

By the end of the nineteenth century, Victorian racism had reached its height, fuelled by the propaganda of psuedo-scientific racism. The James family were to be seriously affected by a particular incident during the 1890s. Edward Sheffield James, Edward's oldest son was approaching his thirteenth birthday when his father summoned him to the kitchen table, where, whenever Edward was home from sea, the week's expenses would be worked out each Friday night.

"Edward", said Edward senior, "you're becoming a young man now, so I'm going to pay you wages for helping your mother in the shop."

Edward was delighted when he was given money, but then his father said, "Oh, one thing. Now that you are a man you must pay your keep to your mother, while I'm away." He promptly took away a portion, but said, "The rest is yours to do as you like with."

Young Edward was naturally delighted and began to think about how to spend his 'wages'.

He was well-known as a dapper little chap, very meticulous about his appearance and hopeful that he would become successful in later life. Edward Sheffield was not to survive his thirteenth birthday for very long. At that time the area of Liverpool now known as 'China town', now famous for eating out, even then had many restaurants, which were not, as now, run by the Chinese community, who were mostly involved in laundry businesses. Edward decided that, more than anything else, he would like to behave like an adult and use his new-found wealth to buy a slap-up meal in a 'swank' restaurant. The owner of the restaurant was not able to fault young

▲ **Edward Sheffield James**

Edward on being inappropriately dressed, nor could he exclude him on grounds of being unable to pay. Edward died some days after in some agony from food-poisoning, the family always believing that he was intentionally poisoned, at least by being given inferior food. The restaurant was not prosecuted, as in those grim days the family did not possess the means.

JOHN ARCHER

Another family was that of John Richard Archer (1863-1932), Mayor of Battersea in 1913 and Britain's first black mayor. John's father, Richard, was a Barbadian ship's steward whilst his mother, Mary Theresa Burns, was Irish born, a frequent union in Liverpool. John spent most of his life in the cause of socialism and his attitude to race appears to have been shaped during his early life in the port. In view of at least some links between the experience of poor whites in Liverpool and the levelling down of all black people, irrespective of former social rank, it is no surprise that John Archer chose to follow in the footsteps of those other black founders of socialism associated with Liverpool, James Brown and William Davidson. John was an altogether different character than William, however, and spent his life advocating equality by peaceful means.

John was born on 8 June and eight years later lived at number 3 Blake Street, behind the present-day Lime Street Station and not far from the infamous Brownlow Hill Workhouse. As a young man, John left Liverpool and travelled at least three times around the world. Living for a while in the West Indies and North America, it was in Canada that he met his wife, Bertha, a black Canadian. After marrying, John returned to Britain, settling in Battersea in the 1890s at 55 Brymaer Road, near Battersea Park. Battersea's political complexion at the time was dominated by the labour, Liberal and radical internationalist movements, which may have encouraged the black couple to settle there. The base of the Anti-Slavery Clapham Sect (see chapter on 'Friends and Allies') had been Battersea, John greatly admiring Granville Sharpe and Thomas Clarkson, who he felt should be honoured for their bold stance in what he called 'the Negro's cause.'

John began his political life speaking against spiritualism, but was soon involved in the Battersea Labour League. As well as being elected councillor, John was well-known for his practical approach to social welfare and was elected to the Wandsworth Union Board of Guardians in 1906. He was a medical student for a time and later John appears to have been a successful photographer, winning many prizes for his work.

In November, 1913, John was nominated for Progressive candidate for Mayor in Battersea amidst a media circus, as T. P. Brogan, had been the first Catholic mayor and John Archer's mentor prior to his election. Due to ignorance of the old Liverpool Black Community and the appearance of people of the old dual heritage Liverpool population, mistakes were made about his origins, many members of the press believing him to be Burmese and showing surprise at his command of the English language. John was elected on 10 November, receiving congratulations from many influential people all over the world, including the Black American activist, W. E. B. Dubois, who stated in his journal, *the Crisis*, that he "fears no man, and brooks no insult because of the race to which he is proud to belong"

He did face appalling racism in some quarters, notably the media. One newspaper printed an item upon his election, 'It is not meet that the white man should be governed and controlled by a man of colour. It has always been that the white man ruled and it must always be so. If not, goodbye to the prestige of Great Britain.' (South Western Star, no 1,873, 7 November 1913, p 5).

John was a close friend of the musician Samuel Coleridge Taylor, the composer of 'Hiawatha', both being black activists and members of the African Association formed in 1897 by students from the Black Diaspora. It comes as a surprise to find the lives of two notable black people overlapping in this way until one considers the smaller black population and very difficult times. Both John and Samuel were elected as representatives to the first Pan-African Conference at Westminster in July 1900. This first all-black conference was organised by Henry Sylvester Williams, a Trinidadian and did in fact, petition Queen Victoria to consider the plight of 'the native races', as they were then called (even by the Pan-African Conference!) The death of Samuel Coleridge Taylor in September 1912, only a year before John Arthur was elected Mayor of Battersea, was described by John as "a blow to the race".[18]

Although John was a Pan-African, believing in a common bond between black people everywhere, he also appears to have adopted the view of the emerging socialists, which recognised links between all disadvantaged groups. Some decades later, Martin Luther King, near the end

▲   This beautiful statuesque woman is Mrs. Emily Orgill, the great-grandmother of Mary Jane Sweeting (1912-1994). Born in Liverpool in the first half of the nineteenth century, Emily's descendants know that she was half Portuguese, but are uncertain where her black parent came from. It is possible that he too was Liverpool-born.

of his life, sought similar links. When John was elected as councillor in Battersea, the black vote was very small indeed.

Keir Hardie and Ramsay MacDonald are better known to the British public as the founding fathers of the Labour Party, but men like the eminent Indian politician Dadabhai Nairoji and John Archer played a notable part.

THE DESCENDANTS OF ROBERT COX

The Liverpool Black ancestors of Laurence Westgarth date back two hundred years. Laurence, assuming the role of family *griot*, has managed to trace the family tree back to a mariner, Robert Cox, who settled in Liverpool in the first quarter of the the nineteenth century.

St. Peter's Parish Church records show the marriage of Robert to Margaret Holland on 12 August 1822. Robert had a brother John whose descendants are also scattered under various surnames in the Liverpool area. Robert's son, Charles Henry Cox, born 1842, married Hannah Stubbs and lived at Stilligoe Terrace in Stanhope Street, the heart of the black community.

Laurence's great-grandmother, Sarah Jane Doughty, was Charles and Hannah's grand - daughter. Sarah Jane married twice, her first marriage was to Jeremiah Jenkins, while her second was to an American named Deabru, who joined the American Navy at one point in his life. Laurence Westgarth, through his mother Carol (Darby) is from this line, whilst his cousin Maria is through the Jenkins line.

The family of settler Henry Brew remember Laurence's Uncle Jerry, son of Jeremiah, as a talented musician who could play a variety of musical instruments. Henry Brew possessed a fine Steinbeck piano of particularly good quality which Jerry Jenkins was asked to tune whenever required. Jerry often enjoyed playing it afterwards, and would show more than ordinary

skill. George Quarless, of another old family, remembers Jerry as having an equally talented brother, Charlie:

"Both were very good guitarists, but I think that they could play anything. They'd often be called upon to play at any parties, but often they'd just start playing -anywhere."

Laurence can trace his Liverpool black roots seven generations with accuracy, but this family could be even older. Little is known about his earliest known female ancestor, Margaret Holland. If, in Laurence's future searches, he discovers a connection with that other black settler, Benjamin Holland, mentioned in Chapter One as being baptised in a batch of three, implying possible slave status, his ancestry will date back to the 1770s.

Despite that particular uncertainty, it is likely that the black Cox family has a connection with Thomas Cox, a member of the Africa Company and a wealthy merchant with a plantation in Jamaica and several slave ships. With the capital he made from the Slave Trade, he bought Sarah Clayton Parr's Collieries in St Helens, a rich coal-field providing fuel for the colonies, Ireland and other parts of Britain, shipped, of course, from Liverpool.[19] Finding precisely what the relationship between the black Cox family and Thomas Cox is likely to be difficult to discover. Even if it is proved that he was the owner of their ancestors, that other relationship, ties of blood, could also be possible. The commonest form of abuse faced by female slaves was sexual, resulting in an astonishing number of modern Western blacks having white ancestry brought about in this way. Following the abolition of the Slave Trade (but not slavery) in 1807, many slave owners found it very convenient to 'breed their own' slaves, as they could no longer buy them. Slavery continued in British territories until 1834 at least, many remote islands, such as Bermuda, not being emancipated until 1838.

THE DESCENDANTS OF ELIZABETH SIMONS

Rachel Freeman, now a great great grandmother, remembers the roots of her own early black family in Liverpool:

▲ **Elizabeth, granddaughter of Elizabeth Simons and grandmother of Rachel Freeman.**

"Starting from the beginning that I can remember, Elizabeth Simons had Clarrisa (Clarrie), Clarrie had Ulrika, my mother. my mother had me and my children had their children - that's a few generations, all black and all born in Liverpool. Elizabeth Simons came at thirteen years of age. She was a stowaway on a ship from Nassau in the Bahamas. It was easily the middle of the 1800s. Instead of the police sending her back, they took her to work in the Liverpool Police home. A ship came in from the Bahamas two years after and the police took her down to the ship to see if anybody recognised her. She got to know a feller on the ship - she was dancing - and she ended up marrying him. His name was Clarke, not related to Jim Clarke. Clarissa, her daughter, married becoming Clarrie Wallace, who had a second Elizabeth.

The second Elizabeth's children were Clarissa, from which the Marshall family are descended; Margarita, who lived in France with Henrietta, who was the origin of the Weaver family; a third Elizabeth; and Ulrika, my mother. My mother, always called Rikka, was only 38 when she died. She was born here. Her own mother was black and she was born here herself- in Caryl Street in 1875.

My Auntie Lizzie was called after my grandmother and great great grandmother. Her married name was Lizzie Wickham, later becoming Lizzie Stephens when she married Uncle Steve. She was a great friend of Alice Quarless, of another old black family.

On my father's side, he was a Lloyd -Evans. He was born in the Gambia. He was descended from a Lloyd-Evans from Wales who married a black woman. His mother was Senegalese His name was Walter Lloyd-Evans and he had a brother, Edward.

I married Thomas Freeman, who was a seaman, he was a Liverpool-born black. His father was only 16 when he came here from Liberia. He was here 12 months when he went to work in Bibby's and stayed there until he was 65.

When I lived in Beaufort Street when I was young, the Archer family lived down that way, possibly cousins to John Archer's family, their ancestor also being from Barbados). So did the Christian Family (the family of George Christian's brother). They used to call the mother 'Biddy' Christian. She had two sisters and they were from Ireland. Biddy's sister was married to Mr. Jones, an African, Charlie Jones, father. Biddy's husband was named Richard and another sister was married to the Coles.

Mary Sweeting, another family friend, was married to Hazelwood, the watchmaker, and they lived over the water. He was a West Indian. She was Alma Marshall's friend. The clock shop, Hazelwood's, was in Great George's Street. Mary Sweeting was from the Gray family, another old family". (See picture of Emily Orgill, an ancestor of the Sweeting family)

▼ **Albert James, son of Bermudan settler Edward James, with his wife Ethel Vernon Jones. He survived the Great War, unlike the many black Liverpudlians who gave their lives for Britain.**

THE COMMUNITY MATURES

Worsening conditions for black people following the mid-19th century affected the lives of the poor most. The sort of social mobility exemplified by the Brown family and individuals such as John Archer and George Christian was the exception rather than the rule. Even talented individuals, such as the young West Indian settler, J. Alexander, found life in Liverpool and the rest of Britain difficult towards the end of the century. Born in St. Vincent, Alexander learned Welsh on the trip to England from the ship's captain, not

only reading, writing and speaking the language as well as English, but singing all the popular Welsh airs upon his arrival in Liverpool. This was to stand him in good stead during the 1870s, enabling him to earn a living as a street-singer in the absence of other employment, literally 'singing for his supper'. Described as being "as black as coal, with teeth like ivory", the youthful Alexander could usually be identified as he walked the main streets of the city centre by his habit of carrying a small black bag and a music book.[20]

Another black street entertainer of the period, Seth Davy, was a West African often seen in the Scotland Road area of the City accompanying his cheerful songs with a dancing puppet show. Although the Park Lane - Stanhope Street - Parliament Street area was the main area of black settlement, over half the black population of approximately 3,000 were, in fact, living in other parts of the port by 1911, though nearly always in the poorest districts.[21] The family of Edward James, indeed, lived in the Dingle area, immediately to the south of the main area of settlement, whilst John Archer was born in Blake Street behind Lime Street Station in the present city centre.[22]

The reduction of wages of African firemen following the seamen's national strike in 1911 was illegally sanctioned by the National Maritime Board, ironically in 1914, when the outbreak of the First World War brought about a great increase in black labour in Great Britain as they came flocking to the "Mother Country" from every part of the empire; brought in to replace Englishmen for national service, taking such jobs as munitions and chemical workers.[23] In the event, blacks were to do much more than this. There was some doubt expressed about allowing blacks to actually fight, but soldiers of the black Empire did, indeed, take part as combat troops, just as they had in the American War of Independence..

Not only did the black Empire rally to Britain's call, but the locally-born community, by this time

▲ **Marcus Bailey with an unknown soldier of the King's Liverpool Regiment. His cap badge shows *'The Chester'***

black Englishmen to all intents and purposes and of several generations standing in some cases, answered the Nation's need. Two sons of Edward James, mentioned earlier, entered the service of their country. The birth certificate of Albert James' daughter, Edith, in 1914, shows him to be one of the first to enlist at the beginning of the War. He served in the Royal Field Artillery,[24] serving in Egypt, Bulgaria and France, whist his brother William served in the Merchant Navy. When Albert signed up, he left a one-year-old son and a wife five months pregnant, such was the pull of patriotism.

Both survived the War, but many black Liverpudlians did not. Pat O'Mara, the "Liverpool Irish Slummy" commented in his autobiography-

"There were few Saturday night celebrations among Flukey Alley's Flukes, Sparling Street's Negroes and the Chinamen of Pitt Street. Even in these un-

British sections tragedy and gloom had deepened for many half-caste boys had lost their lives in the war."[25]

In spite of this early writer's politically incorrect terminology, the message is nevertheless clear that British black people did indeed make their own contribution to the freedoms that the rest of British society would claim to value so much.

The patriotism of people from all the British colonies is summed up by Sierra Leonean-born Ernest Marke near the end of the First World War. Alfred was only fifteen at the time, but remembers standing on the corner of Stanhope Street and Mill Street with a friend, Tommy Macauley, also from Sierra Leone and only eighteen himself. They had seen one of the famous posters depicting Lord Kitchener with the caption saying, "Your country needs you!"

"That's us", said Alfred, and both boys promptly went along to the recruiting station at St. George's Hall. They found themselves in Seaforth Barracks that evening and were later transferred for training to Whitchurch, Shropshire, joining the Preaseth Camp 159th Recruitment Distribution Battalion.[26]

THE BAILEY/BADER FAMILY

The family of Marcus Bailey, a seaman born in Bridgetown, Barbados, 1883, have an astonishing history of service to what they felt to be their country. Marcus married in Fleetwood and found his way to Liverpool, where his three children were born. He served on no less than 34 merchant ships and ships from the fishing fleet before joining the crew of the Royal Naval vessel HMS Chester as an able seaman after receiving his certificate in 1912. HMS *Chester* was known for taking part in the famous battle of Jutland During World War I, during Marcus' service.

Lilian, his daughter was born in Upper Stanhope Street, Liverpool. Lilian was orphaned

◀Geoffrey Bader, Lilian's son, became a helicopter pilot in the Navy.

at nine years of age when Marcus died at a comparatively young age, a blow that caused her to be separated from her two brothers. Lilian was placed in a convent, where she stayed until she was 21, when she entered domestic service for a while. When World War II began to loom, Lilian experienced her first taste of military service in the Naafi at Catterick Camp, Yorkshire. Lilian

▼Lilian's wedding with her handsome tank-driver, Ramsay Bader.

enjoyed it until she was summoned by her superior, who told her in a very apologetic way that he was going to have to dismiss her, as a mistake had been made as her father had not been born in the U.K. After that initial disappointment, it was a while before Lilian heard that although West Indians had been turned down by the army, the R.A.F. were accepting them. Thus it was that Lilian became a W.A.A.F. In those days, if you were black, you were foreign. Lilian says:

"It was a Scots sergeant who looked at our hair. As she tutted at a girl whose hair was obviously not to her liking (having nits), she looked up and saw me. "Ah! she said. "I bet they don't have these where you come from." I was in my own country; she wasn't, but to them I looked foreign. I grinned and felt some of the girls looking at me."

Lilian moved to York, but her stay was saddened by some bad news:

"My brother Jim had been reported missing, but I hoped against hope that he had been picked up as I knew he sailed in convoy. The survivors of the "Western

53

Chief" were picked up, but Jim was not amongst them. We had lost both our parents when I, the youngest, was nine in 1927. I had been rudely torn away and sent to a convent in North Yorkshire. A few letters; they were only young boys after all, a couple of photos, and one visit from them in 1936, were all that I had left of family life. On hearing of Jim's death, I applied for compassionate leave...It is not generally known that merchant seamen were volunteers."

Lilian became a corporal in the RAF and began writing to a handsome young tank driver, Ramsay Bader, also Black British. They married in 1944.

Lilian Bailey had two brothers, James and Frank. James had been killed in action on 14th March 1941 and Frank was later invalided from Royal Navy minesweepers. The tradition of service in the armed forces in this family did not end there, however. Lilian had two sons, Geoffrey and Adrian. Geoffrey joined the Royal Naval Helicopter School at RN Air Station, Culdrose, to learn how to fly helicopters. He received his wings from Admiral Fell and went on to serve on HMS *Osprey*. In doing this, he combined both the service traditions of his family; the Navy and the RAF. With a grandfather and two uncles in the Navy and both parents in the RAF, Geoffrey did not have a chance!

A World War II cartoon from Britain's bleakest hour after Dunkirk, when Britain stood alone against the enemy, might have been equally relevant to World War I. Two 'Tommies' are sitting on the White Cliffs of Dover glumly looking across the English Channel. "So our poor old Empire is alone in the World", says one. "Aye, we are - the whole five hundred million of us.", says the other.

British-born black people were there too.

SOCIAL CHANGE IN THE EIGHTEENTH AND NINETEENTH CENTURIES

THE BLACK POOR

Although not all early black settlers were slaves or the descendants of slaves, the levelling-down effect of the propaganda of the Slave Trade upon all black people settling in Britain meant that most black people were, by and large, to make their homes in the poorer districts of Liverpool. Parish records show this from at least the last quarter of the eighteenth century[1] and from the earliest times a friendship between poor whites and blacks seemed to have formed, often in conditions of abject poverty. In spite of this, a degree of racism was still to be found as even the poorest were still prey to the negative view of black people spread by the plantation owners and others making a living out of the Slave Trade. In Liverpool, the parish registers themselves clearly show that blacks were not considered the equal of their fellow parishioners. At the beginning of the first volume of St. James Baptismal Records of 1775 to 1807, black people are to be found segregated onto a separate page.[2]

As a group, to any large degree, British blacks never presented a serious threat to any particular interest or social group during the nineteenth century.[3] Towards the end of the century the gap between black and white was beginning to widen as Liverpool's black population grew, but the economic rivalry between poor blacks and whites in Liverpool did not reach direct confrontation until the national seamen's strike of 1911, leading to the horror of the 1919 riots following the Great War.[4]

The steady trickle of Irish immigration into Liverpool increased enormously during the 1840s with the Irish potato famine of 1845, reaching disastrous proportions as conditions continued to deteriorate amongst the poor in Ireland well into the 1850s.[5] Flooding the port in their search for work and relief from the conditions in their homeland, the Irish settled in the poorest parts of Liverpool, including the black settlement area, taking the roughest, least skilled jobs, such as building labourers or porters.[6] The difference in their religion appears to have initially caused them almost as much difficulty as black people experienced through their colour, "mixed marriages" between Catholics and Protestants being frowned upon in many quarters.[7] This situation was to change as the nineteenth century progressed, however, as colour became the overriding factor.

Other groups of immigrants to the growing port included many Scots, Italians, Norwegians and Chinese, each, like the black community, having their own settlement areas in various parts of Liverpool. The Italians settled in the north-end of Liverpool (then a township in a cluster of streets later to be given Italian names including Cavour and Mazzini Streets, rebuilt as two tenement blocks known as Cavour and Mazzini Heights. The Scottish settlement was grouped around a public house known as Gregson's Well, though this is of no particular significance insofar as their drinking habits were concerned, as many Scottish settlers were Presbyterians and teetotal! Most Norwegians chose to live amongst the black settlers, like many Irish, having a similar maritime background. The Liverpool Chinese Community, although the earliest in Europe, did not take root until the late nineteenth century, also settling in the oldest black settlement area in the Park Lane district.

By 1852, Liverpool had the largest provincial Jewish community in Britain. In 1842, a synagogue had been founded in Hope Place, near the Stanhope Street district, to accommodate Jewish people living among the Irish and black settlers in that locality. Later in the century, new Jewish immigration from Eastern Europe resulted in an influx of poor peasants desperately in need of assistance from Jews in this country, many of whom were little better off than themselves. A Hebrew Philanthropic Society had been founded in 1811 to help the needy amongst the Anglo-Jewish community, but as the number of immigrants grew, a Liverpool soup kitchen for the Jewish poor and the Society for Clothing the Necessitous Boys of the Hebrew's Educational Institution (founded 1866), plus a Liverpool Hebrew Free Loan Society (1861) were set up originally as ad hoc measures to cope with the human privation.[8]

One writer suggests that black people were often accepted by the English poor, whilst Irish Catholics were often rejected, quoting the tendency of the London mob to aid runaway slaves and black servants, in spite of their usual xenophobia as expressed in their popular chant "no popes, no Jews, no wooden shoes!" (poor Dutch settlers).[9] This could have been true, but the idea of poor whites being more likely to provide hospitality for black settlers may be a myth in itself, based on the persisting image of Liverpool blacks as recent immigrants. The popular notion of black settlers even needing to receive the charity of poor whites in Liverpool may be based on a lack of understanding. In the case of the influx of white settlers from elsewhere during the nineteenth century, the Liverpool black population had already been established for many generations and may sometimes have been in a position to provide at least some sort of shelter to refugees from famine and pogroms even worse off than themselves.

▼ Nineteenth century foreign emigrants setting out for the "Lucania", from the emigrants hostel in Great Georges Square in the area of black settlement. (by Thomas Burke, courtesy of Liverpool City Libraries)

▲ 'Pipes' by Thomas Burke, courtesy of Liverpool City Libraries

THE POOR DIVIDE

Ironically, the camaraderie between poor Liverpool blacks and whites born of a shared experience of hard times was sadly to be eroded by the success of moves towards social democracy during the nineteenth century. The struggle for electoral reform made its first breakthrough in 1832 with the Reform Bill of that year after great civil unrest. Although artisans in the towns and agricultural labourers still remained without the franchise, the thin edge of a wedge had been driven that would widen with Disraeli's Reform Bill of 1867 and Gladstone's Franchise Bill of 1884.[10] The 1867 Reform Bill gave all householders in towns a vote, while the franchise in the counties was given to £12 householders. The Bill of 1884 conferred the franchise on agricultural labourers who were still without a vote.[11]

Many of Liverpool's poor were forced to live in dank cellars, lodgings and rented rooms and,

as such, may not have been considered householders, the necessary voter's qualification, but nevertheless, the inevitability of a schism between poor blacks and whites was already likely. It is unfortunate that the period over which the struggle for universal suffrage took place, at least from the early nineteenth century Chartists to the Bills of the late century universal suffrage (for men, that is; women were to have to wait until 1918) should have run concurrently with changes in how black people were perceived in Britain. With universal suffrage, the white poor were at least provided with the machinery to better their lot. Blacks were not to be so fortunate, in spite of the historical involvement of many eminent black Liverpudlians in the struggle for social justice. By the time of the advent of universal suffrage, the colour of their skin had come to identify them with a servile past and an unflattering image resulting from the prevalent mythology concerning blacks from which they could not escape. With the passing of time and improving conditions of the poor, more poor whites were able to pass into the middle classes. The increasing denial of this facility to poor blacks and, indeed, blacks of higher station as all blacks came to be seen in the same light, undoubtedly led to poor whites distancing themselves from their black fellows as they chose to identify themselves increasingly with the Anglo-Saxon ruling class.

These changes in attitudes towards black people during the nineteenth century led to the levelling-down of all black people living in Great Britain regardless of their original social class in their home countries (or, in the case of Liverpool Blacks, any higher social station they may have earned in British society). Although black people of every rank may have been increasingly identified with the lower orders of British society during the second half of the nineteenth century, this did not automatically provide a comfortable niche within British society. During the Victorian era and the successes of the British Empire, changes in attitudes towards black people were accompanied by the 'lower orders' of British society allying themselves with the middle and upper classes, joined not only by a common Anglo-Saxon ancestry, but even Celtic areas of the British Isles feeling themselves to be subject peoples (not forgetting the large Irish settlement in such English cities as Liverpool), the whiteness of their skin. This was matched in other European dominated countries such as the United States by the flow of immigrants from Europe in the later part of the nineteenth century, whether Czechs, German or Rumanian, also adopting an 'Anglo-Saxon' heritage as a result, in the case of the USA, of an education policy aimed at producing an homogenous nation.[12]

In the late nineteenth century society, not only were the characteristics of the more successful leaders of the all-conquering British Empire emulated by people of lower station when in the company of 'lesser breeds' of humanity, but

▼ **Jim Crow by William Henry Hunt, painted in 1837 (By permission of the Board of Trustees of the National Museums and Galleries on Merseyside (Walker Art Gallery, Liverpool)**

accomplishments in reality beyond the scope of many of the lower classes at this time, such as scientific inventions, literary and artistic works, and higher technological discoveries, were adopted as their own as the greater group feeling grew to embrace all people of European descent. This heightened race feeling during the late Victorian period is sometimes aptly termed "basking in reflected glory" and is similar to the observations of sports psychologists commenting upon the fact that many sports enthusiasts will not only wear the shirts of their favourite team or sports personality, but will even adopt their hairstyles and clothes.

The fact that many poor whites in Liverpool not of Anglo-Saxon origin, such as the large number of Liverpudlians of Irish and Norwegian extraction, were not as hindered as their black counterparts (at least when the tremendous barrier of social class and poverty was overcome) was due entirely to the colour of their skin, a factor that was to ease their assimilation. Many descendants of settlers from other parts of Europe now hold influential positions in present-day Liverpool; doctors, headteachers and politicians, but the Black Community appears as though in a time-warp; "trapped in the prison of their skin." as one young black writer put it.[13]

DAILY LIFE

In spite of increasingly difficult conditions during the nineteenth century, the Liverpool Black Community appears to have shown a remarkable resilience. Reporting on a situation that is depressingly familiar in our own century, Henry Mayhew says of the Liverpool black Community in 1861 -

"It is only common fairness to say that negroes seldom, if ever, shirk work. Their only trouble is to obtain it. Those who have seen the many negroes employed in Liverpool, will know that they are hard-working, patient, and too often underpaid.

▲ A street in the area of black settlement in the nineteenth century

A negro will sweep a crossing, run errands, clean knives and forks, or dig, for a few pence. The few imposters among them are to be found amongst those who go about giving lectures on the horrors of slavery and singing variations of that favoured book "Uncle Tom's Cabin". Negro servants are seldom read of in police reports, and are generally found to give satisfaction to their employers...Whenever they are out of work, they have no scruples, but to go into the streets, take off their hats and beg directly". [14]

Throughout the nineteenth century, the Liverpool Black Community was continually added to by new waves of black settlers following

each of Britain's wars, as citizens of the British Empire answered the call of the Mother Country. This factor has tended to hide the true age of the black community and has helped to perpetuate the popular view of Liverpool Blacks as exotic and un-English. White Liverpudlians and, indeed, the rest of Anglo-Saxon Britain, traditionally have taken the most recent wave of black immigration as representative of the Liverpool Black Community. Black sailors from West Africa and the West Indies played a considerable part in the growth of black settlement in Liverpool. Athough traditionally black seamen were employed as cooks and stewards, the introduction of steam-driven iron-clad ships led to the recruitment of stokers from the West African coast, India and Madagascar, thought to be better suited to the appalling heat below deck. Many stokers presented a pitiful picture. Those who chose to make Liverpool their home were described by an early twentieth century Liverpool writer, recalling his childhood, as -

"...poor thin creatures of all colours equally poorly clad, a common sight in Liverpool. They drove the ships through hot seas. No wonder they were walking skeletons. what a hell it must have been shovelling coal, stoking the furnaces deep in the bellies of the boat. No air conditioning then. Scarcely enough draught with the funnels extended to keep the furnaces going." [15]

The "*Porcupine*", a Liverpool newspaper in 1861, offers a tableau of life in the Liverpool District 1 at that time:

"The houses appear to be crowded with people of a class neither good nor good looking. Sailors and fat frowsy women loll about. A black, with a red shirt and a blue cap, is gambolling for the amusement of a group of girls. Very unpleasant allusions to the eyes and limbs of passers-by are made - the games of the children take tone from what is seen around - the houses are, for the most part, in a state of disorder - and

the notion of Sabbath evening enjoyment, which the children have, is not flattering to those who claim to have them under their pastoral care". [16]

It is always important to take care to note the source of information of this sort, for the writer of this particular piece was at pains to discredit the work of a particular churchman in this locality who obviously had his enemies. This churchman, the Rev. Henry Postance, spent 50 years of his life in Toxteth, building churches, ragged schools and trade schools, [17] including Ashwell Street in 1860, Grafton and Beaufort Street schools in 1868 and a Girls' Industrial School in Nile Street in 1870. [18] The Rev. Postance was appointed to the parish of Holy Trinity, Toxteth Park, in February 1856. Described as "a kind of sediment along the edge of the Queen's and Brunswick Docks", this parish did not possess a church at this time and it was not until the following year that a site was found, the foundation stone being laid on December 1, 1857 and the church opened for services on August 8, 1858. [19]

This unfavourable reference to the life-style of the mixed community of South Liverpool - for the black community has always lived amongst whites, in spite of the ghetto feeling of the area -

might perhaps be balanced by an account by Charles Dickens in the same year, which paints a more sympathetic picture whilst retaining something of the same flavour of poverty. Touring the Toxteth dockland slums with a police superintendent (on a 'pub crawl', in fact!), he chanced upon a public house in which the clientele were predominantly black. On that occasion, the police officer mentioned to Dickens that -

"They generally kept together, these poor fellows......because they were at a disadvantage singly, and liable to slights in the neighbouring streets." [20]

Dickens also commented that the white women in that public house, where "the jovial black landlord presided over a scene of merriment and dancing kept up with childish, good humoured enjoyment" [21] were *the least unlovely, both morally and physically"*, he had seen that night.

It is interesting to note that despite his degree of racial tolerance, in this quotation, Dickens fell victim to the prevalent popular view of black people as child-like figures. An almost contemporary article by Dickens in the "Saturday

◄ **Black street trader at Georges Dock 1895 taken at the end of the 19th century by Charles Frederick Inston (Courtesy of Liverpool City Libraries)**

▲ Canon Postance

number of little children huddled together on the step of a public house. They were barefooted and had scarcely enough clothing to cover their nakedness and crying so bittlerly that they must have been suffering intensely from cold and hunger. None of the passers-by took heed of the little sufferers, possibly because it was a very common sight. I wonder if any of that little group survived their miserable childhood and how many that night sown seeds of disease. Poor innocents of a bestial traffic which had destroyed all sense of parenthood and responsibility in those who should have been their natural protectors." [23]

Review" of January 4, 1862, once again emphasised the idea of the gentle affectionate barbarian or, even more so, the child-like black. [22] Dickens also seems surprised that the white women consorting with black men that night were not necessarily of the lowest order, a stereotypic image still sometimes prevailing in modern society.

CHILDREN

Poverty and alcohol, a panacea against the worse deprivations of life in the poorer parts of Liverpool, often went hand in hand during the late Victorian period. Public houses were to be found on almost every street corner, the worst lasting until the licensing legislation of the early twentieth century. [31] Agnes Cowper described how drink affected the standard of life in the area of black settlement in Liverpool during the 1880s:

"It was a raw winter night, and sleet was falling. As we passed the corner of Dexter Street and St. James' Place, we saw a

Agnes Cowper does not state the race of these particular children, but in spite of poor living conditions common to most poor areas of Liverpool and many other large British cities, the black settlement area did nevertheless maintain a degree of respectability, as Mayhew observed, in some ways above that of many other poor districts. Pitt Street, in the heart of the oldest part of the black settlement area, was considered a street down which a woman might walk without harassment, unlike many other poor areas of the city. This tends to contradict the myths concerning black promiscuity still to be found in popular perceptions of black people. [24]

A doctor, later to become Sir James Kay-Shuttleworth, saw education as a way of combatting poor housing and insanitary conditions. He had trained as a doctor in Edinburgh and had practised in Manchester during the great cholera epidemic of 1832. Dr. Kay was moved by the degradation and squalor to emphasise in his writings that infants were victims of the system. Most were ill-fed and ill-clothed; living in a state of cold and neglect, more than fifty per centy of poor children dying before the age of five. [25]

Dr. Kay's writings inspired a group of influential citizens of Manchester to form the

Statistical Society to carry out an investigation of a sizable portion of the North-West, including Liverpool. In creating the Committee of the Privy Council under Dr. Kay in 1839, Lord John Russell had given the poor a powerful friend and ally.[26] Liverpool, which the Statistical Society showed to have up to one half of its children untouched by educational influences, was also fortunate in having its own pioneer of health in Dr. William Henry Duncan, mentioned in the previous chapter. Overcrowding and poor ventilation was found to be common and Duncan was dismayed at the exhaustion of the many weakly children in the schools. [27]

Following the foundation of the Harrington School in 1814, other schools established by Dissenters in the Liverpool area of black settlement included the Society of Friends (Quakers) Boys School at Duncan Street East (now Hotham Street), in 1819, one at Jordan Street by the Wesleyan Methodists in 1820, Lime Street school, by the Baptists, in 1821, and a further school for infants at Duncan Street East in 1824.[28] Following the Reverend Hesketh's remonstrances

that the nonconformists were doing a good deal more to educate the poor in Liverpool than the Established Church, in 1824 Liverpool Council built two schools out of public funds; one in the North end of the town and one in Park Lane, the heart of the Black Community. Most of the Roman Catholic children preferred to attend the Harrington School, run by the Unitarians, tolerant of most religions, rather than schools run by the Established Church.

The greater part of the black settlers followed the various Christian denominations by this time and Copperas Hill was still the only Catholic school available in 1830, a little too far from the black settlement area.[29] St. Peter's school for Roman Catholic children was established in Seel Street in 1831, to be followed by Norfolk Street in the black settlement area itself, two years later. In 1835, St. Patrick's School was opened in South Chester Street, easing the problem of the education of poor Catholics further, the same year the Church of England opened St. Michael's School in neighbouring Pitt Street.

SMALLER LIVERPOOL.

◀ A sketch of poor Liverpool children, made in the nineteenth century.

Popular education provided a useful implement for the practical implementation of the nation's wishes, or at least those of the ruling class. In November of 1909, just a few years before the Great War was to devastate Europe, the Harrington School in Stanhope Street was issued with a new 'drill' syllabus by the Board of Education. Previously, small apparatus, including dumbbells, barbells and Indian clubs had been used to the accompaniment of a musical instrument, But an ex-army drill sergeant, Sergeant Paterson, was appointed as the School Board's peripatetic drill instructor in 1903. The school's new physical education syllabus was drastically altered, the children now doing exercises without any apparatus, usually taking the form of 'figure marching', arm movements, and military-style drilling, in short just the sort of training needed for what has come to be called 'cannon fodder'; able bodied, disciplined recruits from such areas as Liverpool Districts 8 and 1 already conditioned to army life. [30]

The curriculum of other schools in the Liverpool black settlement area also reflected the heightened patriotism of the time. In nearby St. Peter's School in Seel Street, the ideology of the British Empire was considered an essential part of the children's education. Recalling his schooldays in St. Peter's, one writer commented that the idea of the Empire and its preservation was an essential theme of every school textbook. The reason was never satisfactorily explained, but pride of Empire, the Navy and the necessity of keeping Britannia ruling the waves was considered sacred. [31]

MUSLIM LIVERPOOL

During the late nineteenth century, many Muslim children and other non-Christians usually attended the schools run by the more tolerant Unitarians, such as the Harrington School in Stanhope Street, but even those attending Liverpool's mosque, the only formally recognised Muslim institution in England, were not immune

to a self-indulgent curriculum reflecting the notion of Britain's greatness in the world and the dominance of Western culture. The Liverpool Mosque had an appointed Sheik and Imam and was to be found not in the nautical riverside population, but at Brougham Terrace in West Derby Road, some miles away from the dockland area. The mosque was not custom-built, but appears to have been quite a humble house adorned by a golden star and crescent (until 1999 occupied by the Liverpool Registrar of Births, Deaths and Marriages building). The Imam held religious services on Fridays and each day at noon would call the faithful to prayer using a balcony instead of a minaret. As a mosque, the interior of this house was not unusual; through a Moorish arch could be seen the 'mihrab' or niche indicating the 'Kibla' or direction of Mecca at the eastern end; the 'Mimbar' or pulpit for the sermon and a raised platform from which the Koran was read. Compared with modern British mosques, it was the service itself that seems unusual. Nearly all the hymns were taken from well-known English Christian evangelical poets and divines, the words altered and adapted for the purpose. The congregation would sing with fervour and familiarity to such tunes by Wesley, Cowper, Watts and others, including the hymn, "Abide with me", with the last verse adapted for Muslim worship[32]:

"Abide with me when close these mortal eyes
Shine through the gloom, and point me to the skies!
Heaven's morning breaks, and earth's vain shadows flee;
In life, in death, Allah abide with me!" [33]

This hymn was one of a collection entitled "Hymns suitable for English-speaking Moslem congregations" and even the Christian Religious Tract Society were surprised by this influence being exercised upon Muslims in Liverpool. In 1896, they expressed the view that the Muslim leaders in Liverpool seemed remarkably susceptible to Western and Christian culture, putting it down to the effect of Christian surroundings upon Islam.[34] There is a simpler explanation, however. The Imam at that time was, in fact, W, H. Quilliam (known as Abdul Quilliam), a Manx convert of some means who seems to have become something of a philanthropic benefactor to the Liverpool Muslim community. There does not seem to be any evidence that the Manx Imam was insincere or out to change Islam in any way, as the Liverpool Mosque stood high in the esteem of Muslims abroad and was frequently visited by distinguished visitors. Other leaders were described as "earnest men, and sanguine of the future of their work" [35] and such was the good of the Liverpool Mosque that in the 1890s an endowment was received from the Shahzada of Afghanistan. It is, of course, possible that the worshippers at the mosque were not aware that the tunes of their songs of praise had been plagiarised from Christian hymns by their respected Manx Imam, however well intended. The Liverpool Mosque had more than a hundred members, including children, and it can be seen that even transient visitors, as well as Liverpool born Muslims (the majority being black), could not escape aspects of the somewhat ethnocentric ethos found in the English school curriculum, even, it would seem, in schools they had set up themselves! All Black British pupils, whatever their religion, were as much influenced by this aspect of their education as their white fellows, as shown in an earlier chapter in the reference to "many half-caste boys (sic.) who had lost their lives in the war." [36]

THE DESCENDANTS OF ABRAHAM LAWRENCE

The Quarless', Waylands and Chases are cousins and just part of a well-respected family/ clan in Liverpool descended from Abraham Lawrence.

George Quarless paints a picture of life in the Pitt Street/Upper Frederick Street area at the end of the period of this book:

"In the summer, the men used to congregate in the corner of St. Michael's Church at night time. They'd be talking away, children would be running around and people would be sitting on the doorsteps.

In those days, nobody had such a thing as a fridge. Nearby, we had a big building, Duke Street Cold Storage, and if they were in a good humour, they would give us ice. So, if you knew you were going to get a piece of ice, you'd go home and get a bucket. We used to make drinks with it - ice-cold drinks, with it being hot - and it was hot in the summer holidays. Lemonade drinks, use it with strawberries - things like that.

My father was John Isaac Quarless, a Barbadian sailor born in 1872. He married my mother, Elizabeth Lawrence in the 1800s. I remember when he came home, they used to have this thing by the Pier Head, where the Mersey Dock and Harbour Board offices are. It was a big slate, and the ships coming in to dock would have their names put on that slate; the time of the tide, what time they were coming in, and what dock the ship was going to. We'd go down to the slate when he was expected home to see what time the ship was going to be in, then you could gauge what time he was going to come home. In those days, you very rarely saw a cab outside a person's house, but my dad would get a cab up from the ship with his case. There'd be all kinds of things coming off. There was no oil then for cooking purposes, it was dripping, so there'd be three big cakes of that. There'd be a stack of bananas, not ripe, they'd be green - you couldn't eat them for a while. There'd be coconuts; there'd be African oranges. They were only small, thin skinned, but you'd never get a sour one - dead sweet. That was the first time I had guava jelly, and I still buy it. I knew kids around our way who'd never seen a banana. The only time they'd see bananas was when the fellers used to come around the street with them, and that wasn't very often, or coconuts. Kids around the streets had never seen them.

He was a ship's steward. He'd make bunloaves - he had the tins and everything. He'd make mince pies - they were like a meal on their own. He'd make puddings with those dishcloths with the red edges - he'd make them with them. He'd make one for each of my brothers, great big ones. I used to get fed up with them. You had them with custard, you had them without custard, he used to fry the things! You had plenty of rum in them.

He used to make his own sauces. One of the favourite meals by my dad was salt fish with onion and tomato gravy, with rice and peas. There was another one, but I would never eat it. With cornmeal, with bream, or any kind of fish you want, but I could never stomach the cornmeal.

I remember when my dad was saying that when he was on the sailing ships (in the nineteenth century), the person who did the cooking was the master's wife! He said, "They are talking now about officers taking their wives away, but when I was on sailing ships, the master's wife used to do the cooking!" Imagine that kind of life! He was only young at the time.

Noel Quarless, the boxer, is my brother Harry's grandson. His father was Walter, the musician with the group called 'The In Crowd'.

My dad died when he was 101 years of age in 1973. I was looking for something, I couldn't find it anywhere, and I found a little bit of paper with 1800s on it. My grandfather's wife had died. She came from Shrewsbury. She was in domestic service and my grandfather got in with her and

married her. His name was Abraham Lawrence (a mixed marriage, as Abraham was black). When my grandmother died, at that time my grandfather had a house in Pitt Street, right opposite St. Michael's Church. On the little piece of paper, torn out of the Church Magazine, it says, "Abraham Lawrence lost his wife and he has a daughter who has taken her mother's place in looking after the family." That was my mother, the eldest. Sarah Anne was the youngest and was the last to get married. She married the first Wayland in Liverpool (another old family, therefore cousins to the Quarless') and apparently, my sister was telling me, when she was living with us as one of the family, that was why I never called her 'Auntie Sarah Anne', because we were that close.

Around our way, there were lots of other black families that were old; the Hammonds, the Birches and the MacKenzies, to name just a few.

John Quarless' wife, Elizabeth, was of dual heritage, therefore the black roots of the Quarless family goes back to the first half of the nineteenth century, if not earlier, through George's mother's side, and to the last half of the century on his father's. George's mother had four sisters and a brother, Liza, Harriet, Sarah Ann, Emma and a son, Dwane. Liza was the mother of Alice Martin, who became Alice Chase, through marriage, the mother of Dorothy Chase, the first remembered Liverpool-born black teacher. George is uncertain as to whether Abraham Lawrence was himself born in Liverpool, but this could be the case.

ENTERTAINMENT

Although only very young at the time, Black Liverpudlian Grace Wilkie, now in her eighties, gives an account of efforts to relief the daily grind of black parents and their children at the end of the period of this book:

not formal. They were sometimes just set up in people's rooms. People would agree to meet at a certain point, on a certain date, and that was the club night. On those occasions, there would be a certain amount of drink and socialising and there would be the opportunity to meet the opposite sex.. Following the mid-nineteenth century, attitudes towards black people hardened; black people finding it very difficult to be accepted into white people's homes, find places to go and drink and meet and even places to live. This was the origin of what was to become black clubs and black meeting places.

The most common form of informal club was what young student's now call the 'paying party', called 'sixpenny dances' by the black community in the early days. This was usually brought about by somebody placing a plank across a doorway in a house, each visitor paying a few coppers to the door-keeper. The people who ran these were poor themselves, drink, and perhaps some food, being acquired on 'tick' from a willing public house, and any leftovers being returned.

Rachel Freeman remembers her own early years in the black community, describing the entertainment provided by her own mother and grandmother at the beginning of the present century:

"My mum used to have it - to help the people. They'd move the furniture out into the house next door and they'd have the 'sixpenny dances'. They call them 'shebeens' today, but they weren't then; they were called the sixpenny dances. Powie Wenton used to play the guitar. Powie Wenton was the father of Bernie Wenton, the well known singer - he's been on the television. 'Titmouse' - they used to call him Titmouse - was Mrs. Alcock's brother or cousin who used to play the guitar with him in my mother's sixpenny dances.

Our house was number one Brassey Street on the corner of Beaufort Street. It was a pub turned into a house so it was big. First we lived with my grandmother in Beaufort Street and then this pub came empty,

▲ **This photograph of James and Frank Bailey (see Chapter Three) evokes the spirit of live entertainment common throughout the whole period of this book.**

"In the old days, Liverpool was a main port, with a lot of seamen, here from Africa and the West Indies. They would hold concerts at the African Hostel once a week for the black men's wives and their children, because there wasn't very much for the kids. Some of the mothers would go up and sing, somebody would play music and they'd spend an hour or two getting a cup of tea or coffee or whatever. Sometimes, when a black person died, they'd fund together- they'd take care of all that; the families in distress. They'd do a good job to look after the old people that needed help."

In spite of the image given by Dickens of 'black pubs', many of the early clubs and pubs were

66

▲ Ulrika Lloyd-Evans, Rachel Freeman's mother.

money. And then you'd be back the next night and get it out again. You had no capital! It was always on trust and a sale of return. They wouldn't give it to you if you weren't trusted. They would know you. You'd go to the side door to get the drink.

When I was grown up, I used to go myself to what was then called a shebeen. The shebeen I used to go to was Johnson's, which later became the Mayfair club. That was in number 19 Falkner Square. Before he had a license, he had a shebeen there. Johnson was a Jamaican feller, and then there was Fat Johnny and other shebeens were coming up. When it became easier to get a license, they began licensing them. George Wilkie's club was in Parliament Street.

The first club that everybody went to, black and white, was Joker's on Edge Lane (by

▼ Stephen Cole, television star of the Channel 4 'Brookside' series. son of Irene, Rachel Freeman's daughter.

turned into a house, and my mother moved into there. Now, the stairs came into the living room, so me and my brother would be at the top of the stairs, watching them all dancing! I was only five or six at the time, but they'd been running them like that for a hundered years

Then my mother had the handcart outside the door, where she used to sell fruit, potatoes and veg. Me and our Walter would have to sit on the handles when she'd have to dash into the house for a cup of tea. My mother also used to go around the doors selling fish with a basket on her head. From there, she went to work in Moels as a cleaner, across the water.

The people would buy a drink at the sixpenny dances. It would be a 'sale or return.' from a pub. What didn't get sold, you could take back and cash in for your the mid 20th century). Before Joker opened on Edge Lane, he used to have a gambling house on Great George's Street.

I ended up having my own club, 'the Gladray Club', but that's another story!"

As now, black Liverpudlians were keen on preserving their dignity, planks rarely being placed across the outer door of the house, an inner room or interconnecting rooms being used. This has been put down to the illegality of the shebeen, but black dignity and the preservation of working class respectability was also a factor. The negative 'Hogarthian' image of such improvised paying parties, particularly during the late eighteenth and early nineteenth century, is largely the result of white cartoonists. In reality, even up to the Second World War, people who were down on their luck and unable to pay for entrance to the shebeen were rarely turned away and the tradition of collection for elderly or ill friends was continued. The positive side of shebeens of providing a meeting place for people to find out how other people in the same circumstances were faring has often been played down; black people in the early days (and some would argue, nowadays) having no single organised focus point in physical terms.

THE CONSOLIDATION OF RACISM

The days when a well-born black student living in the house of a wealthy patron in a street like Rodney Street in Liverpool might disregard a black servant because of the difference in their social class were long gone by the end of the nineteenth century. The blackness of the skin of people of African descent had become the overriding factor. Whilst racism shown by individuals may have been the most common, it was institutional racism that limited the life-chances of black people. A group of missionaries en route to Africa passed through Liverpool in 1884, enlisting the help of a local lay churchman, J. H. Brown of the Liverpool-based firm, Fowler Brothers. Brown was asked to provide good hotel accommodation for the group whilst in the port, but soon found that even mention of Africa was enough to bring underlying racist attitudes to the surface. He chose a convenient hotel and told the hotel keeper that accommodation was required for about 40 missionaries on their way to Africa. The response was instantaneous. Brown was told in no uncertain terms that the hotelier "wouldn't allow a lot of niggers to come into his house at all." Brown promptly left and tried "Hurst's Temperance House", receiving a far better response. The hotelier Hurst said that he was very pleased to entertain the missionaries as he did not "stand on colour or nationality, and will entertain a black man just as cheerfully as a white man if he behave himself." When the missionary party arrived, Mr Hurst was surprised to find that there were no black people amongst them. From then on Hurst's hotel was the stopping place of American missionaries passing through Liverpool, black or white, to the annoyance of the hotel owner who had refused to entertain the so-called 'African' fathers.[1]

Racism shown towards black people by individuals nevertheless bit hard and deep. The British-born composer, Samuel Coleridge-Taylor, was descended from a black American loyalist and responsible for such well-known pieces as "Hiawatha's Wedding Feast" and "Symphonic Variations on an African Air", receiving the praise of such notable figures as Elgar and Sir Arthur Sullivan. He was born at a time when everyday life for both black visitors and British blacks was already engaged in a downward spiral and, in spite of his talent, received an astonishing degree of prejudice. During his school days, he was not only nick-named "Coaley" and "Nigger", but on one occasion had his hair set on fire to see if it would burn! Samuel had two children, a son called Hiawatha (b. 1900) after his success, and a daughter named Avril (b. 1903). Both became eminent musicians in their own right; born to his white wife, Jessie, into worse conditions for black people than their father. As a little girl, Samuel's daughter remembered him gripping her hand so hard that it hurt as they were approached by coarse whites shouting abuse. Times were to become very hard for blacks in the Britain of the early twentieth century.[2]

THE BASSEY FAMILY

Although not a Liverpudlian, the experience of Samuel Coleridge-Taylor shows that by the beginning of the twentieth century, even well-educated black people were having to find ways of surviving in an increasingly hostile environment. The shame of returning to the lands of their origin was not an option because of loss of face to relatives who did not have the personal experience of racism in European society. The only avenue open to members of the black student caste was to do precisely what Henry Mayhew had said black people did in the 1860s in Liverpool - swallow their pride and find ways of surviving. Maintaining their dignity was becoming increasingly difficult and many well-born black people were forced to try to hang on to some vestige of dignity. The well-educated Nigerian, Thomas Bassey, arrived in Britain from Calabar in the early twentieth century and is remembered by many as a familiar figure seen in the Granby area, immaculately dressed with bowler hat and brolly, raising his hat in greeting to passers-by; an African gentleman, a contradiction in terms to European eyes. His son, Solomon Bassey, remembers his struggle to come to terms with racism. He was forced to put his good education to the best possible use available:

"He always wanted to be self-sufficient. As long as I've known, we kept chickens. He used to breed chickens. He used to get them a day old and rear them. Then people, his friends, used to come around to buy them. he'd slaughter them and he'd sell them to them. He always wanted to be self-sufficient; not dependent. Obviously, with the size of me now, we never went short of food. He always taught us to be independent and proud, and I think that has come out in us when you look back.

My dad was a strict disciplinarian - very. Sometimes my mum used to say, "You're too strict", but he didn't change. And, I mean, I look back now and I see the way the kids are today and I think, "I've been brought up well!"

When he first came, he became a seaman. Then, later on in life, he became an illegal bookmaker. He could obviously read and write well, and his friends used to come round and he'd write letters for them. He'd buy the air-mail form, which was about two

or three pence. He'd write whatever they'd want and the letter would get back home some way.

Up until he died, he was a bookie's runner. Well, he'd run for the bookie - they were the forerunner of the betting shop. When you think - illegal! - it probably was a big thing in those days, but today it's nothing that you would bother about.

Before the Nigerian club opened, he used to go to meetings. He was involved in that - he died before it was ever opened - but every Sunday, at twelve o'clock, he'd be away with his homberg and his brolly to go to these meetings. People used to say, "Oh, your dad's very proud!", but he always was. Any time he bought a suit, it was a three-piece suit and an extra pair of trousers! It was class, when you look at it. He still had that pride and he used to press

▼ **Thomas Bassey was a member of the educated West African caste, but found life difficult in Liverpool in the early twentieth century.**

70

all his own clothes. I used to have to take his shirts to the Chinese laundry in Crown Street, because he wanted starched collars. The Dove family, another old family, lived next to the Chinese laundry. They had the house at the side. Their dad went to sea and they were always well brought up. That's where, every Monday, I took all his collars and his shirts.

I was proud of my dad. The only thing with me was, he'd take our David amd myself down to T. J. Hughes' for a suit and he'd want to barter! We used to look..... David and me! They'd say, "Oh, we've knocked three pounds off, sir," but it was their way of trading back home, barter. So, he never did anything wrong, and, in fact, today, I've been to Dixons' and I've bartered for goods and I've got it! They've said, "All right, I'll take....", because all that you are doing is taking money off their commission, so you are still bartering. It works!

I used to like him cooking snapper or mackerel with palm oil. If you told people about palm oil today, they wouldn't know it, or okra. He was a brilliant cook. It was hot. That's why I'm into hot food. He used to say to us, "Do you want something to eat?" and you couldn't leave a thing, it didn't matter how hot that food was. And you couldn't touch that water until you'd eaten the food. We were taught not to waste. If you see something and you want it, you've got to eat it, and you couldn't leave until that plate was empty. There was always food, because some of his friends would come around and there was food for them, if they wanted to eat, so even though we were not rich, we had that rich culture.

One of the biggest legacies he's left us is pride, and every one of us can cook - from my sisters to my youngest brother - we can all cook and look after ourselves. He's given us that, I mean, I don't know whether my

kids can boil an egg, but he gave us that and that was great. He'd be proud of my kids today, though. There's my daughter, she's just got a degree in business studies - part time she did it. I said to her when she got the degree, "I wish your grandad was here to see it. He'd have been proud.

I remember when his mate used to come down - Mr Edwards, who died about eight or nine years ago. He used to buy my kids pens when I lived in Entwhistle Heights. He was my dad's friend. He used to buy Sonya a pen and say, "Go and learn!" He had the chemist shop in Parliament Street at one time. He was well educated, too. He used to say to parents, "Don't buy them toys", and he'd give them pens, as well. "Go out, you are better than them", he used to say to my kids.

The thing that struck me was that if you were caught doing anything, your dad's friends could chastise you. They wouldn't chastise you in a bad sort of way, it was just, "Don't you do that in the street." I watch kids today and if they see their dad's mates, they are not interested, but I would be watching for them. They'd say, Next time, I'll tell your dad!" It didn't really matter what country they came from, because he was a very good friend of Mr Kadiri, and he came from somewhere else."

In our time, the new 'credit unions' are currently being seen as the answer to those people whose fortunes do not permit them to take advantage of the normal credit facilities offered by banks for one reason or another, the wrong 'post-code' and poverty being amongst the most common. Throughout the nineteenth and early twentieth century, the Liverpool Black Community experienced this situation with the added factor of colour prejudice. It might surprise some to know that the Black Community's response to poverty and lack of inclusion was to come up with a solution, the forerunner of the modern credit union that, in the tradition of the great Co-operative Movement and other self help initiatives of nineteenth century England, has only recently been rediscovered in our century. Solly remembers -

"When Mr Johnson, over the road from us, used to come home from sea, there were no such things as banks. He'd bring wads of five pound notes, and my dad was a kind of banker for them. He used to hold their money and they'd come to him every day, and ask for such and such to go drinking, so they had that kind of trust in him. Loads of those seamen used to come - he'd still have the little betting thing on. He was the banker for those seamen who had come home, because they didn't trust banks and they didn't want to leave the money in the house, so that was a good sort of trust.

Another thing that I remember about my dad is when he died, Mr. Eyo (Honey Eyo, mentioned in Chapter Two) had insured him and he had insured Mr. Eyo. It must have been from when they first came. When he died, he got the insurance money for my dad. I remember Mr. Eyo giving my mother money, I don't know how much, but he must have collected the insurance money and he came and gave it to my mum. When you think, they must have thought, "We had better insure each other, here, just in case." He must have come over at around the same time.

When the Nigerian Club started, I think they started through throwing their little two and sixpence in every week. How many of them, I don't know, before the Nigerian Club started, because my dad died before it opened, but they must have put their subs

▼ **More recent Liverpool Black family life. Yasmin Bond and youngest daughter, Soraya.**

▲ **Liverpool waterfront in 1896**

there and they must have been banked, because how did they set up, because you get no money off the City Council to open a night club? It was called the Nigerian Social Union and they paid their dues every week. They did well, because if you look at some of the pubs in the area now, they wouldn't serve blacks until 1948, and then you could only go in the bar - right in the middle of the ghetto! I remember a pub in Back Parliament Street. and they didn't serve blacks. They'd say, "We can't serve you."

This system of self-help was not new to Africans. Back home societies had existed within the tribal unit with a very similar role, profits often being used as a form of welfare relief for the needy. Solly's dad was one of a number of West Africans to fill this trusted role. The father of the first black head of Liverpool's Community College, Walter Brown, was a Kru seaman from Liberia, who had the same status, a manifestation of the rank of headman back home. Often sailors would choose someone they trusted from their number, usually better educated, and they would act as a focus for seamen who may never be in port at any one particular time. Sometimes, the 'bankers', would be chosen for traditional reasons, because their countrymen were aware of their rank in their homeland, in spite of the fact that in Britain, one

black was seen to be just as lowly as another!

Solly tells us something more of happier, if struggling, everyday life in Liverpool:

My dad was in Cardiff for a bit. He used to walk down there, on foot, looking for ships, because that was another shipping port. The only ships they got were Palm boats; or Elder Dempster. It was cheap labour for them. It was like the Clan Line, with all Asian labour - just cheap.

When they used to come home from sea, his mates used to bring us tins of sweets, barleysugar and my dad would probably get some cigarettes. They always brought home sacks full of garry, it was in a pillowcase, and the pepper in a bottle and the palm oil. You can't get that food here, well, you can get it now, but you couldn't get it in those days. The friends used to bring it back with them when they had been back home. I look at people now. We used to love pilchards and rice, that was a quick, cheap, meal for us. White people at school used to say, "pilchards! What do you have that for? Their dinner was chips; everything was potato-based with them, and they used to look and say what's that smell? They didn't know what rice was, all they had ever had was rice pudding. It wasn't the thing in those days. I mean you look now and the same people are saying about our food.........Well, rice is one of the biggest things.

Another thing that I remember about my dad was old Mr. See, an old Chinese guy - Alan See's dad- who lived in Carlingford Street, right next door, we were 18 and they lived in number 20. He looked like Ho Chi Min, couldn't speak a word of English, but my dad and him used to hold a conversation; they'd converse together. That was how advanced they were. they could stand together and knew what each other was talking about. Old Mr. See used to go into China Town every day. He used to do all the shopping then he'd come back, but he used to reminded me of Ho Chi Min because he had one of those long beards. The thing was, they used to say that Chinese and blacks didn't get on together, but I am telling you, they did! It's just a fallacy. People like to say, "oh, the Chinese this and that". There were loads of Chinese families around where we lived; there were the Hoys and others.

The Liverpool-born Grace Wilkie gives us a picture of life amongst the black poor at the beginning of the century:

"There was a lot of pawning done in those early days with the seamen and their wives. They would pawn their suit through the week to get food, perhaps for the kids - take it out on a Friday and put it back on a Monday, if there wasn't enough money to feed or whatever. Everybody seemed to be in debt, those that didn't have any jobs, and there were a lot of people like that.

If they couldn't afford the rent, they'd rent a house and they'd live for two or three weeks and skip and get another one, because they couldn't manage on the

Mr. J. C. Archer, a photographer and a man of colour, who is the Progressive nominee for the Mayoralty of Battersea. A close fight is promised next Monday. "I am prepared," he had said, " to meet any man on a public platform on the question of colour prejudice." He had lived in Battersea twenty-three years.

▲ Photograph and contemporary newspaper item by courtesy of Wandsworth Public Libraries

money. I know of some people who used to go hungry because they didn't have enough for the kids. It was so hard to see some kids who had hardly footware enough to keep them warm, their feet would be soaking, especially in the winter - things got worse."

THE 1919 RIOTS

The change brought about by the Great War meant that there was now well-paid employment available for black workers in many parts of Britain; not only Liverpool. The result was that by the conclusion of hostilities, there were something in the region of 20,000 black people in Britain.[3] Favourable employment conditions were unfortunately short-lived and by 1919 many of the Liverpool black community, now swollen to 5,000, were once again facing competition with poor whites, now disillusioned that promises of better conditions of ordinary life in Britain, "homes fit for heroes" had been slow in implementation.[4] By the first quarter of 1921, over a million were unemployed, including ex-soldiers.[5] In this climate, feelings ran high against blacks who, wrongly in the case of the majority of Liverpool blacks, were considered late comers to these shores. White foreign seamen were employed rather than the recently demobilized and indigenous blacks, a situation which prompted a black seaman from Cardiff, that other great port, to write to the Colonial Office -

"We hardly beg to appeal to you for justice. We are seafaring men that have served this country faithfully in her past difficulties either in the service of His Britannic Majesty or in Mercantile Marine. The places of our birth are surely British possessions or protectorates and here in Great Britain which is the Capital of the British Empire we are badly treated by the British people. We do not want any favour all we want is fair play. Every morning we go down to shipping offices to find ourselves work so as to make an honest bread and are bluntly refused on account of our colour, whereas foreigners of all nationality get the preference."[6]

The year after the Great War, a large group of black Liverpudlians employed for many years were sacked by Liverpool's oil mills and sugar refineries because white employees now refused to work with them.[7] This was one of the most deplorable periods in the history of Liverpool Blacks, for in May of 1919 severe riots broke out in which white rioters attacked individual blacks in the streets, their homes, and lodgings, in mobs as large as 10,000.[8] Deaths were inevitable as the hysteria grew and even larger buildings, such as the Elder Dempster shipping line's hostel for black seamen and the David Lewis Hostel for black ratings were sacked. Parliament Street, Chester Street and Stanhope Street were prime targets and many houses were burned in the ensuing orgy of violence.[9]

Grace Wilkie, a toddler at the time, recounts -

"My mother told me, when I began to understand, what had happened during the riots. She said that all the whites and the blacks were fighting. There was cutting, some got arrested and she was compelled at that time to put me in a tin bath - they used tin baths then; because there weren't a lot of bathrooms, and cover me over with blankets and planks to protect me, because they were throwing bottles and bricks, and anything - you name it - through the windows.

It was at this time that Charles Wootton, a young Bermudan seaman, was chased by a large white mob and stoned to death in Georges Dock after leaping in to escape. There was no intervention by police in the vicinity. George Quarless, whose family lived in the same street, says -

"My older sister remembers the time when there were riots on. The family had to go to the 'bridewell' (local gaol) in Argyle Street for safety. That was the night that Charles Wootton got chased and he finished up in the dock."

Many black families were resentful that they were rounded-up and herded into the bridewell for their own safety whether they liked it or not, some feeling that any association with gaol was in some way suggestive of wrong-doing on their part.

Susan Sweeting recalls an indirect injury caused by a family incident during the riots:

"My grandmother's house was in the same area Charles Wootton lived in. She heard the noise going on and heard that a black man was being beaten up and chased. She began to panic, thinking it was her brother that the crowd were trying to lynch and ran out into the street. She left my mother, who was only very young at the time sitting on a chair. With all the noise, my mother must have tried to move, but one way or another, she fell and injured her eye quite badly. All her early photographs show her with a squint, a legacy of the 1919 riots."

Many black families remember that particular night in the same way that Jewish people remember the infamous *Kristallnacht* or 'night of the broken glass' in pre-World War II Germany, when the premises of Jewish people had the windows broken, many being burnt. As in Kristallnacht, the riots were not just a question of one night. Over several weeks many were to suffer, more stories of the riots being included in Chapter Seven, "Friends and Allies".

British blacks had a ready champion in John Archer, one-time Mayor of Battersea and an indigenous black Liverpudlian, mentioned earlier. Archer had been elected in 1913 and was something of a novelty to the press who noted his smart appearance and "his keen contest with an Englishman",[10] failing to recognise the antiquity of the Liverpool black community, an annoyance that has long dogged black Liverpudlians. In a powerful speech to the African Progress Union's inaugural meeting, a few weeks after the end of the war, he complained -

"We are living in stirring times. We have seen the end of the greatest war in the annals of history, a war that marks an epoch in the history of the race. Side by side with the British army, for the first time, our compatriots from Africa, America and the West Indies have been fighting on the fields of France and Flanders against a foreign foe. A war, we have been repeatedly told, for the self-determination of small nations and the freedom of the world from the despotism of German rule[11]... The people in this country are sadly ignorant with reference to the darker races, and our object is to show them that we have given up the idea of becoming hewers of wood and drawers of water, that we claim our rightful place within this Empire. That if we are good enough to be brought to fight the wars of the country we are good enough to receive the benefits of the country." [12]

Black troops had not, in fact, been allowed to take part in London's victory celebrations[13] and the Liverpudlian Archer, in the interest of black unity, did not mention that he had not been brought from anywhere.

▼ **Florence and Mora James as children, whose family descendants could be described, in the words of Mr H. O'Connell in the Houses of Parliament, as being as "British as any Englishman" (photograph taken in the 1880s)**

Life became no easier for black people living in Liverpool during the period between the wars. The city's maritime connections rendered the latter dependent to a large degree upon the fortunes of the British Shipping industry, itself passing through a bad period, part, in fact, of the general world trade slump which limited the chances of industrial migrations in search of other forms of labour. A somewhat out-of-date merchant fleet was competing with less freight, diminishing profits and a highly subsidised foreign trade.[14] Many black seamen, cheaper to employ as stokers and firemen since the national seamen's strike of 1911,[15] continued to be so during the period following the war, but this was of no value to black Liverpudlians domiciled, born or resident in the port in terms of increased chances of employment. Their position was different from black "aliens" (frequently from British colonial countries, in fact, and not strictly foreigners), as they were not favoured any more than their white counterparts owing to the National Maritime Scale from all United Kingdom ports being applied uniformly. Thus, they fell between two stools as black Liverpudlian seamen, born or domiciled, were still nevertheless regarded as an alien force competing for jobs and not fellow union members, a part of the same labouring class.[16] The reduction in the wages of colonial black and brown seamen after 1911 was seen now as militating against the employment of white sailors, leading to a reversal of the Seamen's Union's policy, now pressing for increased pay for black and brown seamen, both in and out of Parliament in the 1920s, complaining of the increasing numbers of alien labourers in industry and the displacement of "British" crews (meaning white) by colonial crews.[17] This campaign was to lead to the Aliens Order of 1920 and the Special Restriction (Coloured Seamen) Order of 1925. Many black Liverpudlians and those from other older black communities such as Cardiff were also required to carry documentary proof of identity along with all black seamen in British ports, despite their British birth and nationality for several generations, and to register with the police as aliens; an injustice based on colour alone. Subterfuge was resorted to, in

actually implementing this legislation, to enforce black seamen to register, such as informing West Indians and other blacks that it was really foreign Arabs that the Act was aimed at.[18] One of the main problems was the use of the word "British" which the majority of the public tended to regard as meaning an Anglo-Saxon member of the Empire.

George Quarless suggests that the institution of 'pass books' was in force a lot earlier than the 'Aliens Order':

"In the first World War, my dad had a pass. They were treated like aliens. You had your fingerprints on them. I've still got his pass somewhere."

The Coloured Seamen's Union, set up in 1936, endeavoured to investigate extreme cases of the misapplication of the Special Restrictions Order. In a description of Cardiff that might well have been the older black settlement of Liverpool, Mr. H. O'Connell, one of its members, commented indignantly in the House of Commons that he had met men as 'British as any Englishman', who had been forced to register as aliens by fraud. He stated (which would have been wrong in Liverpool's case) that they had lived here since the war and claimed that the current ethos, misleading media reports, politicians calling for repatriation and referring to British children as 'halfcastes', could possibly lead to black seamen and their families being expelled from British shipping and the country by trickery.[19]

The difficulties faced by the so-called "half-caste" children were to be the focus of some attention in the late 1920s. Although their presence in Liverpool, as in other ports was ascribed to the increase in black seamen after the war, the fact of black British colonials answering the call of 'King and country' after every British war over the previous two centuries, was forgotten. So was the fact of black people being invited to come to Britain for political, trade and economic reasons, such as the early African students and, in the future, black people from the colonies following World War II. The truth was that the area of black settlement in Liverpool, with its old black presence, was maturing into a dual heritage community with many gradations of colour with, indeed, dual heritage people marrying dual heritage people for several generations as well as simple black-white marriages. Each new wave of black settlers brought new skills, aspects of culture and religions to the growing settlement by the beginning of the twentieth century. The Liverpool Black community was rapidly becoming a distinct people.

CHAPTER SIX

THE BLACK SETTLEMENT AREA

Liverpool takes its name from the ancient tidal creek forming part of the moat around Liverpool Castle (the livered pool or pool with thick water). 'The Pool', covered the present sites of Paradise Street, Canning Place and Whitechapel, but as the size of sailing vessels increased during the seventeenth century, this shallow pool became less suitable as a safe haven for shipping. Prior to the Slave Trade, the borough of Liverpool was little more than an obscure village hugging the west side of Liverpool Castle, now long since vanished. In 1207, King John created Liverpool a borough and a convenient port where men and supplies could be shipped to and from Ireland. The seven streets of the new borough were laid out in the form of a double-armed cross, their names dating from medieval times: Castle Street, High Street, Chapel Street, Oldhall Street, Dale Street, Water Street and Tithebarn Street. To the east of the borough, as much of south Lancashire had become de-forested, King John set aside a large tract of land for hunting called Toxteth, said to be named after a Viking rover named Toki who had been shipwrecked on its shore a couple of centuries earlier. King John enlarged this Royal deer park by adding the adjacent township of Smeedon, whose name still survives in Smithdown Road. A rough road led from the Castle to Toxteth Park, another forking left towards Smeedon.[1] This route defines the present-day black community, the area of black settlement

being linear in character; following the road east from the south shore of the city centre, along the banks of the River Mersey towards the modern built-up district of Toxteth, then winding left up Upper Parliament Street, which eventually becomes Smithdown Road. From its origins in the Old Dock area, the site of the castle, The Liverpool Black settlement area has taken more than two hundred years to work its way towards Mossley Hill, the end of Smithdown Road, never occupying much more than a hundred yards on either side of the road east out of Liverpool.

At various times in its history, the community seems to have chosen different centres at a number of points along this route; an early focus being the Park Lane area. When this became 'overlaid' by new waves of immigration in the form of Chinese, Jewish and Norwegian settlers, the focus became the Hill Street/Stanhope Street area immediately east of what had become the Chinese settlement area. The present recognised focus is the area around Granby Street, midway between the old focus of Park Lane and the most easterly extremity of the black settlement area near the end of Smithdown Road.

Park Lane, later becoming Park Road along its route, was formerly a horse road leading to Toxteth Park, beginning at the ferry at the foot of Water Lane, now South Castle Street. Until the early nineteenth century there were few houses between the road to the park and the parallel River Mersey. Norfolk Street terminated at Simpson Street and green fields sloped down to the south shore. The area of Toxteth Park, now densely populated, was entirely agricultural in the early part of the nineteenth century, there being a few houses, farm dwellings and market-gardeners cottages scattered over the landscape. A mill and dam stood near the bottom of Stanhope Street, a later centre of the black community, then in open countryside. Not far from the nearby St. James Church, built in 1774-1775, was the great quarry between Parliament Street and Duke Street from which stone was obtained for many public buildings in Liverpool. This quarry was to

◄ **View of Liverpool 1791**

become St. James Cemetery in 1829, an old windmill standing where the cemetery chapel now stands and two others at the Parliament Street end of the quarry. Thomas Johnson, Mayor of Liverpool, began an astonishing philanthropic project in 1767 during a winter of particular severity. To relieve the distress of local people, large numbers of men were employed to form an artificial hill, to be called St. James' Mount adjacent to the old quarry. A garden walk called Mount Zion was laid out on this construction to be used as a fashionable promenade for the wealthier local residents.

The earliest black visitors and settlers lived in whichever part of Liverpool the business of their masters or, in the case of black student princes and princesses, their patrons, took them. As the then township of Liverpool was little more than the basic 'H' shape layout of streets it had been for centuries, most black people, like everyone else, lived in what would now be considered the central business district. An early glimpse of a Liverpool street, affording a grim picture of those early poor blacks, was a street nicknamed 'Negro Row' in a late nineteenth century book, "History of the Liverpool Privateers", by Gomer Williams,[2] and probably describes a street with many inns

where slaves were sold at auctions. From this dockland area, the black settlement area gradually moved along the road towards Toxteth Park, now the main settlement area, Park Road passing through what was still essentially heathland with few habitations.

In the last quarter of the eighteenth century, the core of the present black settlement lay outside the present city boundaries. Toxteth Park had no notable population until 1775, when Lord Sefton obtained an Act of Parliament for the letting of building leases. Originally to be called "New Liverpool", the new town was nicknamed "Harrington" after the first Countess of Sefton, daughter of the Earl of Harrington.[3] The township lay roughly between the present Park Street, Sefton Street, Park Road and Parliament Street, named after Lord Sefton's Act of Parliament. All that now remains of the memory of Harrington Town is an Upper Harrington Street and Harrington Dock. Until comparatively recently there was a Harrington County Primary School, known affectionately by older residents as "Arry Board", now closed down as a result of the shrinking population of the area.

Liverpool's wealth may have been built upon

the African Trade and the high seas, but little percolated down to the lowest classes other than through the influx of sailors with money in their pockets to the poor districts as the ships came in. A writer in 1823, contrasting the wealth of public buildings with the surrounding areas of Liverpool, commented that his heart turned in disgust from many streets which presented a spectacle of vileness and misery so strong as to almost overpower any feeling of commiseration or sympathy.[4]

In Liverpool, from a total population of 60,000 in 1793[5] by the 1840s 175,000 souls were estimated to belong to the working class alone. By 1847, as a result of the Potato Famine in Ireland of previous years, as many as 80,000 poor Irish had settled in Liverpool (though as many as 300,000 passed through the port) filling at least 3,000 cellars already officially closed under the provision of the 1842 Health Act.[6]

THE URBANISATION OF LIVERPOOL

Although Liverpool's growth was beginning to accelerate in the first half of the nineteenth century, many areas near what is now the City Centre were still rural in character, largely fields and wasteland, including Upper Parliament Street and Princes Road area of the present day black settlement. The southern end of the town preserved its rural appearance for a much longer period than the north end of Liverpool. Princes Road, now part of the black settlement area, was laid out in 1843, and was bordered on either sides by fields, which for years after remained in a more or less ragged condition, with some of the land occupied by squatters living in wooden tenements.[7] When the Princes Road area was developed, Princes Avenue, originally a suburb of Liverpool with houses built for the "well-to-do" classes; merchants, diplomatic corps and high level civil servants, was also known as Princes Boulevard, electricity line book records, and early Gore's directories of the area giving an idea of

the status of the area's residents. Planned and laid out in the 1860s by speculative builders who wanted maximum profits, the grand houses of the main 'boulevard' providing an imposing public facade hiding the workers' terraced housing still in existence. Built mostly by Welsh builders and contractors between 1846 and 1914, the side streets were intended to house a white working class neighbourhood of less affluent families, possibly in domestic service at the grand Princes Avenue mansions. As the city's wealth improved their lot in life, the wave of migration happening within Liverpool transformed such areas as former residents moved out to more spacious developing suburbs. The vacuum created was filled by socially mobile immigrants from more Southerly immigrant areas, such as many Eastern European Jewish and Polish families, from the Princes Park, Upper Parliament Street and later on Granby areas, rapidly becoming known as a middle class multi-national neighbourhood with a concentration of immigrants.[8]

Later, the old Somali and Lascar, (Yemeni) seamen's community became centered on the Parliament Street area, whilst a Greek community, also linked with shipping trades also had boarding houses in the area. A substantial Welsh community lived in the area and, to this day, an established Irish population.[9]

The area known as Toxteth has amorphous boundaries taking in neighbourhoods such as Dingle, to the south, parts of the Smithdown Road-Lodge Lane-Ullet Road triangle, further east, and parts of the Abercromby /Canning ward areas not constituting part of the University of Liverpool precinct to the west. Rather than having physical boundaries, both the Black Community's and their white neighbour's perception of the geographical area has played an important place in defining its perimeters, an example being the invisible 'chalk line' that has traditionally existed down the centre of Park Road, dividing the poor white community of the Dingle from the poor black community. Interestingly, both communities are in Toxteth. In spite of these demarcations,

▲ A nineteenth century
Liverpool court.

individual blacks live in the Dingle area (and always have) and the black community has always been a mixed community, as stressed elsewhere in this book.

The streets leading onto or ringing the three main parks, (Toxteth, Princes, and Sefton) were planned in a similar manner to Princes Road and Avenue as the spacious homes of some of Liverpool's most wealthy influential families. Strict restrictions on land usage and the disallowing of public houses or shops in the area by the planners and corporation ensured the exclusive nature of these streets and high concentration of religious institutions, some of which are architectural masterpieces with 'Grade

One-listed' status, including the Synagogue, Greek Orthodox church, and some of the Protestant church buildings (added to by the Al Rahma mosque on Mulgrave Street, opened in 1974 and not, as yet, a listed building).[10]

BUILDING A BETTER ENVIRONMENT

There was, however, another Liverpool. As Liverpool became more built up as the century progressed, the port's total population growing from 80,000 in 1801 to 482,000 in 1861, [11] an outstanding figure was to emerge to meet the increase in the resulting health problems. Dr. William Henry Duncan [1805-1909), was concerned particularly with the 'bad effluvias' caused by the living conditions of Liverpool's poor and believed in the 'miasma' theory of the transmission of communicable diseases.[12] Death by consumption among children was one in six during just three of the years over which the research took place. Duncan firmly believed that the construction and ventilation of the dwellings in which the majority of the population lived was critical. For the poorest residents, in 1844, the cellars were ten or twelve feet square and were generally flagged. They frequently had only bare earth for a floor and were sometimes less than six feet in height. They frequently had no window, so that light and air could only gain access to the cellars by the door, the top of which was often no higher than the level of the street. Sometimes a back cellar would be used as a sleeping compartment with no direct communication with the external atmosphere, and receiving what supply of light and air from the first apartment.[13] Publicising his views through papers read before the Literacy and Philosophical Society of Liverpool and directly to the Town Council and magistrates, Dr. Duncan claimed that the construction of the dwellings, lack of toilets and receptacles for refuse and excrement, absence of drains, deficient sewerage and overcrowding was playing a large part in the increasing mortality in the City.[14]

Dr. Duncan's work contributed greatly towards the passing of Liverpool Sanitary Act (usually spelt "Sanatory") in 1846 which influenced the drafting of the Public Health Act of 1848. It was subsequently amended a number of times in the following years as in practice

▶**A street in the black settlement area in the nineteenth century.**

of all, lasting well into the 1860s. A local newspaper in 1861 paints a picture of the black settlement area at that time:

"Anyone who doubts what paving has to do with the appearance of the street, should go into Croston Street, which runs from Parliament Street into Stanhope Street. This is in St. Barnabas district - is narrow, wretchedly paved, and even on a fine Sunday evening like this, is filthy to an unaccountable degree." [17]

This article provides a glimpse of the great undertaking of improving Liverpool's streets and housing, pioneered by such men as Dr. Duncan, showing clearly that in 1861 the work was far from complete. The typical dwelling in poorer areas of Liverpool were known as 'courts'. They usually consisted of two rows of terraced houses placed opposite to each other with an intervening space of from 9 to 15 feet, with two to eight houses in each row. The small courtyard communicated with the street by a passage or archway about three feet wide. The other end of the court would be closed by a high wall or by the back or side of an adjoining building. Most of the numerous courts in the township were cul-de-sacs of this sort, often with poor circulation of air, considered so important by the good Dr. Duncan. [18] The work of improving the worst living conditions was to

some aspects of the Act were not easy to implement. [15] Dr. Duncan's appointment in 1847 as Liverpool's first Medical Officer of Health enabled him to see the terms of the Public Health Act of 1848 carried out, but, even so, his efforts were not able to prevent the cholera epidemic of 1854 [16] which was to hit the poorest areas most

◀**Granby Street c 1906**

▲ A side-street group in the black settlement area 1896

last many decades, the last courts in Liverpool being demolished as late as 1960.

The black settlement in Liverpool originally centred around the South Dock area of the city increased from the mid 18th century onwards, ships engaged in coastal trade with Africa, China and South East Asia docking in this area. Some shipping lines such as the Elder Dempster Line and the Blue Funnel line built their own sailors' lodging houses in the South Docks area to provide accommodation for sailors whose contracts terminated when they reached Liverpool. These lodgings supplemented the private lodging houses and accommodation in the homes of countrymen and kinsmen already settled in Liverpool. Most of the black population in the late 18th century still lived in close proximity to available work, invariably associated with shipping and near those areas of the city perceived as safe for black people to walk and socialise without fear, like the many foreign residents living in special boarding houses

located in mixed residential, multi-cultural, neighbourhoods. The 'better off' classes lived in the then newly developing suburbs of Liverpool and had little cause or little interest to be in the South Docks area, black people in Liverpool up to Duke Street being isolated, both spatially and socially, with little contact with the established Liverpool society.[19]

The physical environment of the black community was to stay fairly static for many decades following the period of this study, if one ignores the aging and disrepair of many of the buildings. With the onset of World War II, the community in the South Docks felt the effects of Blitz-damage to the already poor quality housing in the area, causing a re-shaping of the black settlement as the displaced population migrated to housing along both sides of Parliament Street in the wake of some better off families already moving up between the Wars. Following World War II, black residence continued to spread up Parliament Street, and westwards into properties within the University of Liverpool Precinct. By this time black residents had begun to move into the Granby and Lodge Lane area of Toxteth, most of the previous occupants, Jewish, Polish and other migrant groups moving to the suburban areas of Childwall and Allerton, although a number of Jewish residents remained in the shops and terraced houses for some decades.[20] The Granby Street area, laid out to a gridiron pattern, is the present-day focus of the Liverpool Black Community which now stretches almost from the Park Lane and Dingle area of Liverpool in the south to the City's Wavertree area in the east. The Dingle area is a largely white working-class district now separating the Black Community from the docks in a broad band of similar housing. Separated from the area of black settlement by the invisible boundary of Park Road, the Dingle area represents poorer white settlers from Ireland and other parts of the British Isles who occupy the former dockland home of black Liverpudlians throughout the eighteenth and nineteenth centuries.

In the Granby area during the first three quarters of the twentieth century, attitudes of landlords did not differ significantly from the nineteenth century. Flats owned by the previous white immigrant population from Europe who had purchased poor quality property in varying states of dereliction could often provide a profit if sublet and rented until the council served a demolition or compulsory renovation order. This situation existed for many decades, alongside rented rooms in multiple occupancy houses with minimal amenities sometimes provided by clubs established by former immigrants to meet the needs of more recent, often desperate, countrymen.[21]

In view of the centuries-old tradition of black students settling in Liverpool, the proximity of the University of Liverpool, founded as a University College in 1882, may well have influenced the development of the mixed multi-ethnic community in the adjacent Toxteth area, as many black students, former students, and the descendants of students, still live in the neighbourhood. The prominence of Liverpool in the African Trade had predetermined its role for the education of the children of African rulers and black students (not only from West Africa, but from America and the West Indies) who continued to come to Britain for their education during the nineteenth century. As the nineteenth century progressed, the end of slavery and the subsequent decline in interest in Africa (at least until the onset of the Colonial Period at the end of the century) brought about a shift in black scholarship from Liverpool to other parts of the country, notably Scotland and London which continued to maintain its established role as a centre of black education. The Scottish universities and the University of London plus some medical schools and Inns of Court, seem to have attracted most black students before the last quarter century.[22] Black roots in Liverpool proved too deep, however, and with the growth of the new "redbrick" universities towards the end of the century, Liverpool was once more to see an increased number of black students in her colleges and on her streets. They were often drawn by bonds of kinship,[23] the city becoming the logical choice for something of a resurrection of black scholarship. In "Negroes in Britain", Little gives the earliest entry of West Indian and West African students as 1909, based on a personal communication with the registrar of Liverpool University.[24] This is incorrect, as a students' club known as the Ethiopian Progressive Association had been in existence in Liverpool since 1906.[25] In the years preceding World War II, the neighbouring area to the University campus had a mix of ethnic minority residents, students and others, in cheap rented 'bedsits', in multiple occupancy housing in the once-grand three storey

▶ Canning Dock, showing Strand Street in the nineteenth century. Taken at the end of the 19th century by Charles Frederick Inston (Courtesy of Liverpool City Libraries)

Georgian terrace houses in which middle class families enjoyed the entire property.[26]

THE POST-WORLD WAR I COMMUNITY

The majority of the black residents in the University area eventually moved voluntarily or were relocated to the adjacent Granby/Toxteth area which by the 1950s was being transformed as the middle-to-working class white population moved out in response to the perceived threat of the increase in black residents. As a result, this area has the largest multiracial population in Liverpool.[27]

By this time, the grand facades of Toxteth's main streets and the elegant terraced side-streets had fallen into a state of disrepair. Liverpool City Council, in common with most English industrial cities, put in operation its slum clearance plans, including the re-housing and redevelopment of the South Dock area which had absorbed a large, predominantly poor immigrant population between the two World Wars. Efforts to relocate black residents to more predominantly white working class areas were often rejected, because of the threat of racial harassment, and, similarly, as the outward migration of the white middle class from the Granby area was completed, black residents and immigrants who could not afford better accommodation moved into the multiple occupancy bedsit apartments.[28]

What followed was a period when the black population seemed to accept the status quo for quite a time, preferring the relative safety of Toxteth, equalled only by a complacency on the part of local government. This period was deceptive, culminating in an unprecedented outpouring of anger in the form of the infamous Toxteth riots of 1981, when, for many onlookers, it seemed that all the resentments of the past two centuries met in a few days of total anarchy. Then, after reaching what seemed to be a climax, the area settled down, the Liverpool Black Community continuing in the peaceable way that commentators have reported for centuries as though nothing had happened.

With the advent of European funding, and a tremendous spirit of self-help abroad in the black community since the American black freedom movement, an important phase in the history of the Liverpool Black Community, a new period could well be dawning. The physical environment of the Granby/Toxteth area has recently undergone, and is still undergoing, a period of great change at the time of writing. By one means or another, the spirit of that community has to be retained.

FRIENDS AND ALLIES

Peter Fryer prefaced his ground-breaking work, "Staying Power", with a quotation from the West Indian writer, C. L. R. James, stressing that black people had always had friends and allies in Britain throughout history from the beginnings of the Slave Trade to the present day.[1]

Although the Liverpool Black Community became "ghettoised", it has never become a true ghetto due, to a large extent, to the fact that white immigrants from Ireland and various parts of Europe (not to mention Chinese immigrants from Hong Kong) found homes within the already existing black settlement, boosting the numbers of the local white population. This had a bearing upon relations between black and white; marriages between Irish, Norwegian, Chinese and people of African descent occurred, a degree of empathy existed, and, even as recently as the 1981 Riots in Liverpool, however negative the violence may have been, as many whites were involved as black in what was wrongly called a "race riot". Throughout the history of the Liverpool Black Community, it would seem that there have always been whites of all social stations who have allied themselves, sometimes at great risk, with the Black Community.

As in the case of the young African princes who were often kidnapped and sold, during the

period of African Slavery, any black person ran the risk of being sold, legally or illegally. The Slave Trade itself ended in 1807, enforced by the British Royal Navy, though the abolition of all slavery did not end in British territories until 1834. In 1809, nine black Liverpudlian sailors had been detained by a Portuguese ship's captain and temporarily put in a local prison for safe-keeping until he sailed for Brazil, where he planned to sell them as slaves. The abolitionist William Roscoe and his friends heard about this and put up bail for the men, but the ship's captain and Portuguese crewmen got wind of this and surrounded the jail to claim the black sailors as their own. The black seamen's white fellow prisoners stood by them and insisted that they should not be taken and the Portuguese were forced to retreat, leaving the men alone. The next day, the local magistrates forced the captain to drop his claim and pay all costs. One sailor, not in as good health as the rest, was given a job aboard a ship belonging to William Roscoe, whilst the rest joined the Royal Navy as soon as they were freed.[2]

This is not the only case of poor whites supporting black friends, or, in some cases, even strangers, who shared their day to day existence. The free Liverpool Black Community seemed to have been in constant danger throughout the period of the Slave Trade. In 1859, the Board of Trade took the unusual step of issuing a warning to ships' captains in all ports of the dangers that still existed in such ports as those in the United States (whose own Slavery laws were to last until 1866), incidentally acknowledging the existence of the Liverpool Black Community and British blacks in general. This was the result of a series of incidents over a number of previous decades involving the imprisonment of black sailors. In the Southern States, 63 black British sailors had been imprisoned in the year 1852, and later the same number were forced to seek protection aboard a French ship in New York harbour during the anticonscription riots in New York in 1863. As in the time of the early African princes, one sort of black was felt by those countries still engaged in slavery to be as good as another. Whether they happened to be already free, did not seem to matter.[3]

Black sailors generally seemed to have had the sympathy of the English population in the seaports, although this was to become seriously affected by the seamen's stikes at the beginning of the twentieth century. In 1857, black sailors were told that an American ship recruiting seamen in Liverpool was bound for Antigua in the Caribbean, when in fact it was headed for the Port of Mobile in the deep south of the USA. When the sailors found this out, they realised they had been duped, knowing only too well by this time what happened to black seamen in the Southern States. When a fight broke out between the black crewmen and their white officers, court room spectators were openly sympathetic to the local

▼ **Florence James with a white friend in the 1890s**

black sailors at the resulting magistrate's hearing, even the local press taking the side of the crew against the American officers.[4]

Agnes Brew remembered an experience which took place during the 1919 Riots in Liverpool:

"I was walking along Park Road with a white girl when a gang of men began calling things across the road to me. They started to get nasty and began to run towards us.

Now when I say they were a gang, I don't mean a gang of lads - they were men, I mean, about thirty odd or forty. We started to run, but we both had those dresses that, in those days, were tight-waisted and tight at the knee, so we couldn't. The men began to gain on us and we didn't know what to do.

Well, the girl I was with was very refined - she was a vicar's daughter - but on this occasion she stopped, looked around and picked up a brick. She turned and threw it at the first of the men who were gaining on us. It hit him on the head and bounced off. When the rest saw that he'd been hurt, they stopped to see to him and we were able to get away. I always remember that girl."

The Sierra Leonean-born Ernest Marke had several similar experiences at the time of the Riots. Ernest was visiting friends in the Brownlow Hill area with a West Indian friend when a crowd began shouting "Niggers, niggers. Stop them niggers." The two black youths were fortunate as a white woman heard the shouting and opened her front door to beckon to them. They ran through the house and out the back. after working their way through the back lanes to the tram stops by the Adelphi Hotel. There things began to go wrong. Another gang spotted them and began chasing them. Ernest managed to jump on a passing tram, but his friend was not so lucky. The

▲William Wilberforce 1759-1833

had the protection of the tough athletic Alexander Falconbridge of Bristol, an ex-ship's captain turned abolitionist who always carried two pistols thrust down his belt, but on one remarkable occasion, Clarkson had an attempt made on his life when he was alone. Clarkson was standing at the Pier Head in Liverpool when a gang of ruffians crowded in on him, intending to push him off the edge of the pier. Suddenly aware of his danger, he managed to break through by knocking one down amidst a torrent of blows and abuse.[6] These thugs were not "muggers" or rather "footpads", as they were called in those days. They were paid assassins, or, as we would say, "contract killers", paid by their wealthy masters with interests in the Slave Trade.

THE EDUCATION OF THE LIVERPOOL BLACK COMMUNITY

Liverpool's own "Clapham Sect"

Granville Sharp's reputation as an abolitionist was respected by many British philanthropists, including the Quakers and the London group of friends and neighbours known as the "Clapham Sect", a loose alliance of like-minded people whose influence upon the education of black people, both on the West African Coast and in Great Britain was to be of great importance.[7] The banker Henry Thornton, a director of the later Sierra Leone Company, James Stephen the elder, Henry and John Venn and William Wilberforce, belonged to the Clapham Sect; the inclusion of Wilberforce demonstrating the relationship that often existed between politics and private enterprise.

When Zachary Macauley, another member of the Clapham Sect, who had been governor of Sierra Leone Colony between 1797 and 1798, finally left Africa to return to England on 4th April, 1799[8] he brought some 30 or 40 African children for a European education, much to the chagrin of critics such as Cobbet, who accused

gang of white ruffians caught him and beat him unconscious, leaving him for dead.

Ernest had another lucky escape a few days later. He was popping around the corner to the local grocer's shop with a black friend when they ran into a mob of hooligans. They turned to run back to the house, but ran into a second gang behind them. Ernest and his friend were beaten up mercilessly until some women came out of a nearby factory at lunch hour. They ran at the mob, screaming and shouting madly, fighting off the bullies, who decided to leave the two black youths alone. Ernest felt that their intervention saved his life and that of his friend.[5]

It was not only the lower classes who took risks. White people of all social classes supporting the cause of the Abolition of Slavery were in danger of losing their lives. When Thomas Clarkson visited Liverpool to collect evidence for the Abolitionist cause, he found himself in dangerous situations more than once. In the inns and taverns around Liverpool, Clarkson usually

89

◀ The birth-place of William Roscoe in **Mount Pleasant**

his scheme of "Negro pampering".[9] Macauley had been supervising their education in the colony and managed to persuade the directors of the Sierra Leone Company to support the children, including the boys and girls from "up country" and some children of the previously mentioned Nova Scotian free black settlers.[10]

It is interesting that even the philanthropic abolitionist Clapham Sect were not entirely free of at least a degree of prejudice. When the wife of the black ex-ruler of Haiti, Henri Christophe, was exiled in England, most of the Clapham Sect shrank from admitting her and her daughters into Society. William Wilberforce himself claimed to have no time to spare, his wife not having the 'spirits' to share with them. Thomas Clarkson, of the whole group, appears to have been the only one to offer hospitality, having been begged by Wilberforce to take on the responsibility, much to the relief of Macaulay who commented to his wife that she should feel no apprehension about Madame Christophe, as she was unlikely to come near their family. He did concede that he had no doubt that her daughters were modest and virtuous and that his wife could rest at ease on

◀ In this picture taken in the 1880s of Harrington Board School, there is a lone black pupil. Both Harrington and St. Cleopas were in the Dingle area, just south of the black settlement area, which had few black families at the time.

▶ St. Cleopas Infant School, 1886. The single black pupil is the daughter of Bermudan settler Edward James.

the issue of their mother's morals.[11]

Excluded from Parliamentary and municipal elections, the older dissenters found solace in the part they were to play in the social development of the growing industrial towns.[12] The Quakers, Independents, and not least the Unitarians, applied themselves to the improvement of such ventures as education, public health, hospital building and street lighting.

In Liverpool, one of the earliest philanthropic schools of any size in the area of black settlement was "The Harrington Free School for the Education of Poor Children in Toxteth Park", founded in 1814.[13] The school's founder, the Rev. John Yates, not surprisingly, was a religious dissenter; a Unitarian, in fact, and one of a band of energetic philanthropists who were barred from political office through their religious beliefs until the repeal of the Test and Corporation Act in 1828. Even ministers of the established church, such as the Rev. W. Hesketh of St. Michael's, Toxteth, also in the area of black settlement, were moved to comment on the absence of educational provision compared with the work of Dissenters.[14] The Reverend Hesketh left behind a very proud legacy of tolerance in the Park Lane area, as, to this day, there has always been a good relationship between St. Michael's and the surrounding churches of other denominations.

The evidence points to the existence of a "Harrington Sect"; a Liverpool group parallel to, and contemporaneous with the London-based Clapham Sect. The connection between the early Liverpool educationalist, John Yates, and the London Abolitionists of the Clapham Sect, appears to have been strong. When the Society for the Abolition of the African Slave Trade made its first appearance in Liverpool in 1788, Gomer Williams, writing in 1897, comments that whilst the rest of the town's inhabitants grew fat on the sale of slaves...

"... it appears that there were eight righteous persons still left in Liverpool, who had not bowed the knee to Baal." [15]

He was, in fact referring to the list of members of the Society, published in 1897:

	£	s	d
"Anonymous, Liverpool	2.	2.	0.
Dr. Jonathan Binns , Liverpool			
Mr. Daniel Daulby, Liverpool			
Mr. William Rathbone, Liverpool			
Mr. William Rathbone, Junr., Liverpool			
Mr. William Roscoe, Liverpool			
Mr. William William Wallace			
John Yates, Liverpool" [16]			

When Thomas Clarkson and Alexander

Falconbridge, both of the Clapham Sect, visited Liverpool on their fact-finding mission for the Abolitionist cause, Clarkson called upon Dr. Binns, William Roscoe and William Rathbone, all of whom appear upon the list of Liverpool Abolitionists with the Rev. John Yates. Just as members of the Clapham Sect in London appear to have been neighbours, living within close proximity of one another, so it would seem with the Liverpool Abolitionists. Yates lived at Dingle Head, a large house in Toxteth Park[17] (now the 'Turner Homes), Roscoe, at one stage of his life, in Mount Pleasant, Liverpool,[18] whilst Rathbone lived in Liver Street, later moving to Cornhill adjacent to the area of black settlement. Contact between the Liverpool and London Abolitionists seems to have been close and mutually beneficial. Selina, the daughter of Zachary Macauley, whose interest in the education of blacks has been observed, lived at Dingle Bank, a large house near John Yates' residence at Dingle Head, until her death in 1858 [graveyard inscription. Toxteth Cemetery, grave N. 541, Section L]. Selina Macaulay's gravestone reads -

"Sacred to the
memory of
Selina
daughter of
ZACHARY MACAULAY ESQ.
Who died August 28th 1858
At Dingle Bank, Liverpool
Aged 50 years"

The Swedenborgian Abolitionist Carl Bernard Wadstrom was in fact introduced to Clarkson by William Rathbone during the former's visit to the port.[19] A number of the Rathbone family appear on the lists of subscribers to Yate's Free School in 1818 (Third annual report of the Harrington Free School, op cit) alongside another notable abolitionist, James Cropper.[20]

UTILITARIANISM

The earliest provision for the education of

black slaves and servants contained, alongside a modicum of religion, a very strong element of "usefulness" to the master. This was by no means restricted to poor blacks, free or slaves, particularly after the eighteenth century, when Britain was becoming an industrialised nation. It affected whites as well. The breakdown of feudal ties with the onset of the industrial revolution meant a change in the social structure that would replace the previous sense of duty and responsibility in the relationship between gentry and the lower classes with a master-employee relationship based on wage-labour. [21]

This change was met in Britain by two related philosophies at the beginning of the nineteenth century: that of laissez-faire economics and Utilitarianism. Adam Smith was the leading exponent of laissez-faire economics which was chiefly concerned with 'efficiency' whilst the Utilitarians, led by Jeremy Bentham, John Stuart Mill and James Mill, were concerned with the happiness of the greatest number. The minimum of governmental interference was considered to be beneficial to the new industrial social order with one of the notable exceptions being education, seen as the tool for the institution of the new order.[22]

The Utilitarian belief was in efficiency, every bit as strong as that of the advocates of laissez-faire, and the goal of order and stability, which could be achieved through a stratified curriculum with different sorts of education for each class of society. According to Utilitarian thought, the education of the middle classes should be aimed at teaching the requirements of leadership, whilst cheap and efficient instruction with the emphasis on obedience was thought to be appropriate for the lower orders.[23]

As the influence of Utilitarian ideas of education was felt throughout the nineteenth and even twentieth centuries, the criteria of 'usefulness' was a common factor in the education of both black and white poor. Bearing the above parallel in mind, it is not surprising that schools employing the Bell and Lancaster Monitorial system should also have been especially favoured for the education of young black student visitors, the same criterion of usefulness being not only employed in Britain, but her colonies and proto-colonies.

The statistical society was formed by a group of influential citizens of Manchester, who, inspired by Dr. Kay's writings, carried out an investigation of a sizable portion of the North-West, including Liverpool. In creating the Committee of the Privy Council under Dr.Kay in 1839, Lord John Russell had given the poor of that borough a powerful friend and ally.[24] Liverpool, which the statistical society showed to have up to one half of its children untouched by educational influences, was also fortunate in having its own pioneer of health in Dr. William Henry Duncan (1805-1909). He showed in his researches in 1838 that even the health of children who had not reached school age was affected by conditions in schools in Liverpool, as they frequently accompanied older siblings in the classroom. Overcrowding and poor ventilation was found to be common and Duncan was dismayed at the filth and ignorance of the teachers and the exhaustion of the weakly children.[25]

Following the foundation of the Harrington School in 1814, other schools established by dissenters in the Liverpool area of black settlement included the Society of Friends boys' school at Duncan Street East (now Hotham Street), in 1819, one at Jordan Street by the Wesleyan Methodists in 1820, Lime Street, by the Baptists in 1821, and a further school for infants at Duncan Street East in 1824.[26]

Following the Rev. Hesketh's remonstrances that the nonconformists were doing a good deal more to educate the poor in Liverpool than the Established Church, in 1824 Liverpool Council built two schools out of public funds, one in the North End of the town and one in Park Lane, the heart of the black community.[27]

In both schools, Dr. Bell's module system was employed. The children being taught the Church Catechism, attended an Establishment Church, and made use of the Authorised Version of the Bible.[28] At this time, very few Roman Catholic children attended, most preferring the Harrington (Unitarian) School. The greater part of the black settlers followed the various Christian denominations by this time' and Copperas Hill was

FIRST DAY AT SCHOOL

These photographs were taken on the first day at school of James White and Soraya Bond.

Soraya is the fifth generation of black settlers in this country and James has the same name as one of the original Black Loyalists who founded the Sierra Leone Colony.

still the only Catholic school available in 1830, a little too far from the black settlement area.[29] St. Peter's school for Roman Catholic children was established in Seel Street in 1831 to be followed by Norfolk Street School in the black settlement area itself, two years later. In 1835, St. Patrick's School was opened in South Chester Street, easing the problem of the education of poor Catholics further. The same year the Church of England opened St.Michael's School in neighbouring Pitt Street.[30]

From a relative point of view, Liverpool was soon to be outstanding for its provision of infants schools, the first in Liverpool being opened in Jordan Street in 1823 by the Wesleyan Methodists. Robert Owen, Samuel Wilderspin, James Buchanan and D. G. Goyder, national pioneers of infant education, were all connected with Liverpool. Given this and the connection between the Clapham Sect and Liverpool's philanthropists having already been suggested earlier, it comes

as no surprise that infants schools should have been set up by the Unitarians at Harrington and by a private individual, all members of South Liverpool's version of the "Clapham Sect".[31] Another connection was the fact that, like Wadstrom, Goyder, Buchanan and Wilderspin were Swedenborgians,[32] a group committed to replacing the Slave Trade with "Legitimate Trade", by which they meant such commodities as produce and palm oil.

THE SCHOOL CURRICULUM

Although evidence of a degree of segregation has been observed in methods of recording birth deaths and marriages in at least one church in the area of black settlement at the beginning of the nineteenth century, there would appear to be little evidence of the children of black settlers being excluded from neighbourhood schools which opened later in the century. However, with the

▼ **Empire Day at Harrington Board School in the early 1900s**

deterioration of the European image of black people as the century progressed, integration into the education system was to prove to have as many disadvantages as advantages for black pupils insofar as their own self-image was concerned, in spite of well-meaning friends and allies of the black community. Although writing at a later date, the black American writer Carter G. Woodson felt that the effects of this aspect of European, and American education with its Anglo-Saxon bias, could be detrimental to blacks of the Diaspora, pointing out that black children are encouraged to admire the Hebrews, Greek, Latin and Teuton, but are taught to despise their own race; the notion of black inferiority being sometimes inwittingly drilled into him or her as part of a hidden curriculum.[33]

The curriculum of most schools in the Liverpool black settlement area also reflected the heightened patriotism of the time. In nearby St.Peters School in Seel Street, the ideology of the British Empire was considered an essential part of the children's education. Recalling his schooldays at St.Peters, Pat O'Mara comments in his "Autobiography of a Liverpool Irish Slummy" -

The Empire and the sacredness of its preservation ran through every textbook like a leit - motif. Our navy and the necessity of keeping Britannia ruling the waves is the rather indelible mark left on my memory - though the reason for this was never satisfactorily explained. Pride in our vast and far flung colonies and the need for their protection and preservation were emphasised, as was the confidence that in any crisis the colonies and the Motherland stand as one."[34]

That British black pupils should be as much influenced by this aspect of their education as their white schoolmates is borne out in Chapter Three in which O'Mara remembers the "many half-caste boys (who) had lost their lives in the war". In spite of this loyalty, Law points out that linked

to the prevalent philosophy behind the notion of Empire was the implication of white supremacy which played a large part in intensifying racial feelings.[35] What originally had begun as an ad hoc propaganda measure by the West Indian planters had developed into institutional practice through the years, added to by new theories of black inferiority as new reasons for the promulgation of that myth emerged.

Grace Wilkie, mentioned later, was born in Liverpool at the end of our period and remembers her own schooldays:

"We did learn a little bit about the produce and so on. We were made to believe that all black people lived in little wooden huts. That was some of the teaching I had, in fact I believe that some people still believe that. My uncle told me that it wasn't so. He said that some people lived in the bush, but they did have cities for people to live in."

Solly Bassey, the son of an educated African on hard times, suggests that little seemed to have changed since the period of this book by the time of his own schooldays twenty years later:

At school, I guessed my dad was better educated than some of the other kids, because of the things we used to talk about. We had daily papers - I don't think we had a Sunday paper. I can't remember one, but I know it wasn't the "News of the World". Their dads just didn't mention some of the things. We used to say, our dad's done this and that, and they were kind of shocked that a black man could do anything. There were only four of us in the class, three with Nigerian dads and one, Jimmy O'Loughlin, with a Jamaican dad. They give you the impression that Jamaicans came over at a certain time; they believe that Jamaicans only came in the late fifties, but they've been here for ages.

There was racism, but we overcame that.

They never taught black history! They taught the British Empire and those books, history books, with the slave with the bone through his nose - "This is a savage." We were supposed to take all this in, as usual! I remember when we were going to school, any trips to factories or to the Philharmonic, all the blacks were withdrawn - they couldn't go, they made an excuse. They tried to hide you! "Oh, there's blacks in that school!", if you know what I mean.

As mentioned earlier, Carter G.Woodson felt that the road along which Western education had taken blacks of the Diaspora was less than beneficial to blacks as a people. Although Woodson was an American writing in the 1930s of the education of the race, what is particularly revealing is the growing sense of nationhood, or at least brotherhood between blacks everywhere, a forerunner of the Black Freedom Movement. In many ways this Pan-Africanism, from its beginnings at the end of the nineteenth century, was a counter to the rising tide of white racism. It was to provide links between black people of Africa, U.S.A., the Caribbean and British blacks of such old communities as Liverpool, as exemplified by the Liverpool-born John Archer who was to represent British blacks at the first Pan-African Congress in 1919.[36]

WIVES AND MOTHERS

Not the least of the friends and allies of the black community are those white women who cast in their lot not only with their black husbands, but the rest of the black community, as, once the choice was made, former friends and family often had to be put behind them in the face of social rejection. As the majority of black settlers in Liverpool were male (only 3 out of 34 can be seen to be women in St. James Parish Registers), from the earliest times there appears to have been a good deal of intermarriage with white women.[37] The resulting growth of a dual heritage population

incensed many of the West Indian planters visiting the port, as did the general increase of a locally-born black community.[38] A degree of hypocrisy can be detected insofar as the increase of what they called 'tawny children' is concerned, as their own children born of black women back in the West Indies had helped to swell the ranks of the offspring of wealthy African kings and nobles sent to Britain to receive a Western education. Relations between black and white in Liverpool appear, on the whole, to have been better at the very least than those of Anglo-Saxon dominated America. Herman Melville, the author of 'Moby Dick', writing in the 1820s, observed -

"Speaking of negroes, recalls the looks of interest with which negro sailors are regarded when they walk the Liverpool streets. In Liverpool indeed, the negro steps with a prouder pace and lifts his head like a man; for here no such exaggerated feelings exists in respect to him, as in America. Three or four times I encountered our black steward, dressed very handsomely and arm in arm with a good looking woman. In New York such a couple would have been mobbed in three minutes, and the steward would have been lucky to escape with whole limbs. Owing to the friendly reception extended to them, and the numerous unwanted immunities they enjoy in Liverpool, the black cooks and stewards of American ships are very much attached to the place and like to make voyages to it." [39]

With the hardening of attitudes towards black people as the nineteenth century progressed, negative influences could even be found in views expressed by churchmen.[40] By the beginning of the twentieth century, the right of Anglo-Saxon might had become well ensconced in everyday life. Addressing the first meeting of the Liverpool board of the Eugenics Society, under its new title "The Liverpool Hereditary Society" in 1920, the Rev. James Hamilton expressed his belief in the eminence of the British nation over others by virtue of inherited powers and "...its own great, common blood-stream, always differing more or less from all others".[41] He believed that if the British Empire was the product of national characteristics, then the source of that power should be kept free...

"...as far as possible from pollution, and, especially from certain foreign admixtures... if, for example, the policy of keeping an open door for every foreigner, and especially allowing such alien and inferior breeds as Negroes, Chinese, and Japanese to enter, marry and settle down in great numbers, while young people of pure British blood emigrate to other lands, this country will in a few generations have so much foreign and undesirable blood in the national veins as cannot fail to have a deleterious effect on the national character, and, as a consequence, on all those national ideals, endeavours, and achievements which we value so highly in the present day."[42]

Such rhetoric passing into common parlance was destined to reduce the quality of life for many visitors and settlers fitting the description of "inferior breeds" in such cities as Liverpool and Cardiff. Members of the Liverpool Hereditary Society clearly had such old multi-racial settlements in mind, for at the beginning of the same year the complaint was made that -

"At a meeting of the Public Morals Committee of Cardiff, which took place in February, the Rev. George Hopper stated that he had received several requests to solemnize marriages between white girls and men of colour, and had refused to have anything to do with these matches. Mr. Hopper is a Wesleyan minister whose church is located in Bute Town, the part of Cardiff which is inhabited largely by aliens."[43]

There is, however, another view of the life of seafaring members of the black community which presents a less bleak image.

"Not only where these ugly tribal scarred fellows from the West Coast of Africa accepted by white women as equals; many times they were considered the white man's superior. The main reason, of course, was economic - they made better pater familiae. Some families like my mothers abhorred the practice of intermarriage, but it was so prevalent that they had to keep their beliefs to themselves...The fact that most of the black fellows followed the sea had much to do with the local girls marrying them - much better, reasoned the girls, to put up with a negro three months of the year (while drawing his steady salary) than to marry a young dock walloper and be continually starved and beaten."[44]

This is still a very cynical view of black/white marriages, however. Frank Anti of the Churches Action For Racial Equality (C.A.R.E.), says,

"Why is it that nobody ever mentions love?- there's a book called that! It's funny, isn't it. People are always finding reasons why people of different races marry, but they don't seem to realise that most come about in much the same way as any other relationships - in the first place people simply being attracted to one another, then forming a genuine affection as their relationship grows. Why should they be any different than anyone else?"

An example of this is the marriage of Edward James and Harriet Gates in 1873 mentioned in Chapter Three. Agnes Brew, the youngest daughter of eight children of the Bermudian settler Edward James and in her late eighties at the time, spoke in the 1970s of her parent's relationship in the nineteenth century:

" When my mother was dying [in the 1920s], she was nearing the end when she

suddenly perked up and stared at the end of the bed. A big smile appeared on her face and she said, "Edward!". She said that she could see a little face. By this time my father had been dead for some years [he died in 1913, in fact]. Shortly afterwards, she died, but seemed happy that she had seen her husband again.

I remember that we had this little ship in a bottle. My father had made it himself - lots of the old sailors did. What he'd do is to make a little ship, then fasten the masts. Then he'd flatten them to get them in the bottle and pull them up again by pulling a piece of string when it was inside the bottle. I don't know what happened to it, but he'd made the smoke in the funnel from his own curly grey hair [at the end of the nineteen century, ships were driven by both sail *and* steam]. Well, one day, no-one could find it and my mother was very upset. I suppose it was because of him using his own hair. It must have reminded her of him."

THE WILKIE FAMILY

The lineage of the Liverpool Wilkie family provides not only an insight into the fate of some white wives, but an astonishing slant on the relationship between some philanthropic families and black people. Grace Wilkie, born in Liverpool in the first quarter of the twentieth century has an intriguing tale:

"I'm an old lady now, and if I did go away from Liverpool, I'd be leaving something behind. I was born here and raised a family. I'm raising my second lot of grandchildren. I can't leave Liverpool at all, because I'm unwilling to leave any of the kids. I belong to Liverpool and it belongs to me.

My mother's entire family were white and my father was black. I don't remember much about him, but that he went off to

America when I was a baby. My ancestors were the Croppers of Dingle Bank (a large house that once stood in South Liverpool) an old Liverpool family. They were involved in slavery. They went to Jamaica and wherever slaves were being sold they bought slaves, not because they wanted them for slaves, but they did bring them here to this country and release them and find work for them.

My mother was Elizabeth Cropper. When she married an African seaman, some of her family didn't seem to want to carry on that family tradition. You could say that we were rejected by the family, one half of it. Particularly those who used to come around to my mother, but they didn't want to know when she died when I was ten years old, so I was left with my uncle from Africa. He taught me how to wash, to clean the house, to cook, everything he said that they did in Africa to teach a woman how to grow up, He used to go away to sea also. He used to go on the mail boats for six weeks, then return. The part of it that we liked when we were kids was to go down and meet the mail boats. We used to wait and then pile this fruit, coconuts, sometimes he'd bring a monkey, but they used to sell them.

Years ago, you hardly saw a black girl courting with a white boy, but now they have become together. You see it so often - you go into town, you go to the park, wherever you go - and my mother being white, for me it's the same thing as her being with my father.

My Uncle Tom, on my mother's side, he was white. I used to go in the back alley - or back entry, as some would call it - if I wanted to visit my other uncle."

Whilst touching upon issues of Liverpool Black identity, Grace provides the final twist to the saga of British Slavery. Not only were plantation owners having children to their own slaves, but it would seem that at least one Abolitionist's family had also made that final link with the African peoples they had befriended. The evil of the Slave Trade, which began by dividing human beings, denying a section their humanity at all, had ended with Abolitionist, master and slave becoming as one. The physical leap has been the easiest, since the earliest times of the sexual slavery of black women; the mental connection has taken a lot longer.

"Some were composers of music or writers of poetry.

Others were endowed with wealth and strength, living peacefully in their homes.

All these won fame in their own generation and were the pride of their times.

Some there were who have left a name behind them to be commemorated in story.

There are others who are unremembered; they are dead, and it is as though they had never existed, as though they had never been born or left children to succeed them."

THE NEW ENGLISH BIBLE WITH APOCRYPHA, 1970, OXFORD UNIVERSITY PRESS, CAMBRIDGE UNIVERSITY PRESS, ECCLESIASTICUS Ch. 44 Vs 5-9

This is the tale of the early roots of the present-day Liverpool Black Community. Armed with this knowledge, the question is where to go next in the search for a greater understanding of black people in Britain.

One of the difficulties faced by the Liverpool Black Community is a lack of recognition of its antiquity, both nationally and locally. As a result, it fails to be seen as a part of British society in the same way that other groups have been assimilated. In this book, I hope a number of myths have been destroyed. This process of misinformation began quite early and seems to have had a strange continuity. One of the most prevalent myths is the belief that because of middle-class disdain for blacks, black settlers had to rely on the sympathy of the lower classes in finding dwellings in the poorer parts of the then township; a sort of fellow-feeling amongst the lower classes. The opposite is true, as the first black people ever to set foot in Liverpool lived in the houses of the rich, or at least the comfortable merchant classes. Black people in the early eighteenth century were either black servants living in the homes of their masters or the sons and daughters of African rulers living as equals at least, but more often recognised as being of a higher social class than the merchants and ship's captains with whom they lived. Later, when poorer black people had settled in Liverpool, it is more likely that earlier black settlers would provide makeshift accommodation for poor whites arriving from other parts of Britain and Europe. An example of this, of course, is Irish settlers following the Potato Famine of the 1840s, many of whom found homes amongst black settlers who at the time had lived for at least a hundred years in what was to become the Toxteth district.

When I first began writing this book, I believed that of all the many groups that had made Liverpool their home - the Irish, Norwegians, Italians, Scots, Welsh, Germans, Chinese, Asians and Jews - black settlers had been the group that, more than any other, had remained ghettoised. As seen in earlier chapters, all groups had been ghettoised in nineteenth century Liverpool as new immigrants came to stay with kinfolk and friends from 'the old country'. It seemed that, because of the colour of their skin, white groups have had the facility to become assimilated into the surrounding population, causing the dissolution of their original 'ghettoes.' As I investigated further, however, I discovered that this view was too simplistic. Such an old black population has undergone a good deal of intermarriage, causing some families, such as that of the Bermudan seaman Edward James mentioned earlier, to have descendants ranging from African appearance to apparently completely white, according to marriages throughout two centuries. It became clear that the Liverpool Black Community was by no means isolated and had contributed as much to the genetic gene-bank, as well as the intellectual growth, inventions, political, social, military and artistic development, not only of Liverpool, but the rest of the country, as any other immigrant group. A truer perception might be that those who had retained the skin-colour of their African ancestors were more likely to remain in the old settlement area, whilst some had become so European in appearance that, even in those cases where they were loyal to their black roots, the door was at least open should they wish to leave the area. In Liverpool, black family loyalty is high and this option of 'passing', as the Americans call it, rarely happens, but the option was undeniable in a society where racism and lack of inclusion is still on the agenda.

Two important messages are learned by both black and white from the unique history of the Liverpool Black presence. There is no such thing as a separate, 'old', black community, distinct from newer black immigrants settling in the port; the history of black settlement in the port being a continuous process, ever changing; the latest addition being the Somali refugees settling in Liverpool. Neither should it be thought of black people descended from those first, early, settlers as being people who have lost their original culture, language and religion and are therefore in any way an inferior people, less pure than newer settlers. The old Liverpool Black Settlement has a rich history, being a people quite literally older than the United States of America, with heroes, heroines, tragedies and successes; from James Brown, serving on *HMS Victory* at the Battle of Trafalgar nearer the beginning of the period covered by this book, to Marcus Bailey, serving on *HMS Chester* at the Battle of Jutland at the end of our period.

Successes have been the hardest to attain, because of the still-present spectre of racism. The paper invisibility of Liverpool Blacks has

contributed considerably to their problems of identification. When Liverpool Education Authority was asked to provide information on the number of black children in Liverpool schools by a Select Committee in 1973, the figure was not believed to be true as only the number of 'immigrant/coloured' children was requested, leaving out those children who, like many of their parents, were born in this country. The 1981 and 1991 census presented the same problem as even knowledge of the grandparents of Liverpool Black people did not show their racial origin if they themselves had been born in Great Britain.

The absence of Liverpool Blacks (by far the City's largest racial minority group), a physical invisibility, can also be seen by any visitor to shops in Liverpool's central business district, a reflection of the historic difficulty faced by Liverpool Black people in gaining employment and the acceptance of society in general. The question arises: "Does this invisibility of a section of society of the population matter to either the community in question or society at large?" There is a good deal of evidence to suggest that invisibility has hindered the Liverpool Black Community materially in terms of grants and moves to implement equal opportunity programmes as it has often remained unrecognised owing to its antiquity, many Liverpool black people being undifferentiated from the greater population in terms of language, religion or culture. As well as any material deprivation experienced by the Liverpool Black population, the invisibility of Liverpool Blacks could be seen as a loss to British society in general and a serious setback to racial integration as it perpetuates two myths; one being that black immigration is a recent phenomenon, another myth dispelled in this book; and the other that assimilation and acculturation can cure all of society's problems of racism.

In 1985, the Swann Report expressed their belief that Liverpool Black children had fared worse educationally than any other group with the exception of travellers' children. Many schools have struggled valiantly since then to counter racism and its effects, but finding positive role figures relating directly to British black pupils has often been difficult, as most of the positive imagery comes from the United States or pioneering 'Black Studies' books about remote African kings or other, often too distant, role-figures. In the absence of relevant role figures, black Liverpudlians have had to resort to finding role figures elsewhere. Young black children follow overseas black heroes in the field of sport, politics and music, learn Caribbean patois, and follow black American fashions. This is hardly surprising, as, of all other black people of the African diaspora, African Americans would seem to be the nearest in terms of their needs, place within an Anglo-dominated culture, and, in the case of some black Liverpudlians of Loyalist descent, their actual ancestry.

The time may have finally come for a recognition of the concept of not simply Black British, that idea being a relic of the colonial era, but of a section of British society as being as English (let alone British!) as people of Norman ancestry at the time of the battle of Crecy, the time-span from the battle of Hastings in 1066 to Crecy in 1346 being comparable to the period of black settlement in Liverpool. It should not be thought that members of the Liverpool Black Community in some way crave acceptance, as can be seen by their finding spiritual succour from black people elsewhere in the rest of the Black Diaspora. It would seem to be simply an issue of common justice. Those who do know of the existence of this invisible people might suppose that their presence, though vaguely 'old', is not more than a generation or so, in common with other black settlements in Britain following the two World Wars. The fact of the presence of an almost homogenous people, eking out their existence in poverty, like the children's characters in authoress Mary Norton's "Borrowers",[1] a secret underculture in a state of suppression for two centuries or more, might well come as a surprise to many Britons in the rest of the country.

What is alarming is that through omission as a factor in the hidden curriculum as it affects the education of black people, many of the Liverpool Black population know as little about their own heritage as white Liverpudlians. Black children in Britain continue to experience not only the exclusion of their culture from the school curriculum, but more importantly to British-born blacks, role-models of their race as represented by historic notables such as, in the case of Liverpool Blacks, Britain's first black mayor and pioneer of the Labour Movement, John Archer, mentioned in this study. The impact of this might be lost upon the casual observer, but the effect upon not only the black, but the white, pupil learning how blacks are perceived in their society could be critical. As a result of the exclusion of their history, the older black presence and their contribution to British history has been lost to a large extent; as though such old communities as Liverpool have never existed.

One of the difficulties in supporting the needs of Black British children is that it is becoming increasingly difficult for teachers to become innovators, taking part in the sort of developmental research necessary to bring about change in areas that clearly demand it, such as the unique position of the Liverpool Black school population. More than that, many teachers perceive themselves as being increasingly restricted in what they teach at all. Teachers feel that they are becoming mere technicians, administering a politically ordained preset syllabus. If this is the case, then other agencies clearly must not only supply that necessary information, but provide evidence for politicians to support those educational needs.

In the case of the Liverpool Black population, the most obvious source is the community itself. This book was written as part of that spirit of self-help to aid, in turn, teachers in their daily struggle to meet children's needs, not by being a textbook for children's use, but a staffroom source of information for teachers themselves and the general public. If it succeeds in that aim, then it will be a part of an old tradition that is little known in itself, namely that all the moves to bring about any improvement in the black experience, including the Abolition of Slavery, have by no means been exclusively reliant upon the good works, as undoubtedly they were, of the friends and allies of the black community commented upon in the previous chapter. Throughout the whole period since the early days of the Slave Trade and initial contact with Africans, black people themselves have fought to improve their own lot. To readers in general, I simply ask them to read the story of the Liverpool Black Community and enjoy it.

In this study, the evidence is strong that the academic achievement of Liverpool Black settlers and their descendants has been attained in struggle. If the dictum that schools cannot solve all of society's problems is accepted, the justice of the belief that schools should nevertheless take a positive role and at least some part in that struggle as friends and allies is self-evident. The results of the Western education of black people of those areas of British influence in Africa and the West Indies, now deciding their own destinies, are yet to be seen, as indeed, are the effects of the hidden curriculum which teaches a subtle diminution of the culture and history of black people to students who have received their education more directly in Britain itself. Liverpool Blacks, as a people, along with other British blacks have been forced to recognise their own worth, even if others do not and the question remains of who is to teach them that self-love. The importance of self-love, not in the egotistical sense, but rather the black child's own appreciation of his or her own worth as a human being in a world sadly teaching another lesson, may be as critical to human existence as food and drink. For those teachers endeavouring to eliminate the worse effects of racism in such British cities as Liverpool, the positive role of the education authority is important. In the 1950s and 60s, black people were seen as the 'problem' in regions of Britain receiving any number for the first time.[2] Liverpool with its old black community is a case history proving that any problems of a large section of its black people are not language, religion or culture, believed widely to be the case in the 1960s, as much as European racism.

Many readers may welcome the opportunity to draw together the threads of information which help to clear the uncertainty surrounding the origins and questions of nationality of some Liverpool Blacks already known to them and enjoyed through the media. Actors whose origins may be unclear include Craig Charles of television's *Red Dwarf* fame, who bears the surname of an American Black Loyalist, and Steven Cole, mentioned in this book as playing Leo Johnson in television's *Brookside* series, whose ancestry includes both the Cole family, through his father, Clifford Cole, and the old Liverpool Black Freeman family, through his mother Irene. There is also a secondary Liverpool Black diaspora throughout the world. The American actress, Halle Berry, was Liverpool born, being just one case of the many black Americans who, ironically when one considers their role in the establishment of the Liverpool Black Community, have part of their roots in Liverpool.

Liverpool Black people have a long and proud history of scholarship; from those early black students, lonely figures visiting Britain's shores, often to die in a foreign land, to the present-day descendants of black settlers, faced with a different sort of death and struggling to maintain pride in their own identity. In this book we have seen heroes, eminents, soldiers, sailors and other less prominent members of the community who have nevertheless made an important contribution to British society. It is hoped that it has been shown that Liverpool Black people and, indeed, other Black British, are not incomplete, impure and unfulfilled West Indians, Africans or Black Americans, though they are proud of their descent from all of these. Better that they should be respected as a part of British society whose composition does not differ in character nor history from fellow Britons, who may be descended from Celts, European Jews, Anglo-Saxons, Scandinavians, Flemings, French Huguenots or Normans.

BIBLIOGRAPHY

CHAPTER ONE

THE GROWTH OF THE LIVERPOOL BLACK COMMUNITY

1. Fryer, P. (1985), Staying Power - The History of Black People in Britain, London, Pluto Press, p. xi

2. Williams, G. (1897), History of the Liverpool Privateers, London, William Heinemann, p.473

3. Ibid., p.469

4. "Dicky Sam" (1884), Liverpool and Slavery, Liverpool, Scouse Press, Reprinted 1984, p. 102

5. Williams, E. (1972), British Historians and the West Indies, London, Anthony Deutsch, p. 34

6. Priestley, M. (1969), West African Trade and Coast Society - A Family Study, London, Oxford University Press, p.3

7. Ibid., pp. 7-8

8. Wadström, C. B. (1794), An Essay on Colonization Particularly Applied to the Western Coast of Africa with some free thought on cultivation and commerce, Vol. 1, reprinted 1968, Newton Abbot: David and Charles (Publishers)Ltd., pp. 94-95

9. Law, I. and Henfrey, J. (1981), A History of Race and Racism in Liverpool 1660-1970, Liverpool Merseyside Community Relations Council, op. cit., p.14, after Shyllon, 1974, p.51.

10. Williams, G., op. cit., pp. 372-373

11. Shyllon, F. O. (1974), Black Slaves in Britain, London, Oxford University Press, p. 181-182.

12. Williams, G., op. cit., pp. 524-525

13. Fryer, op. cit., p 60 after Curtin, P. (1965), The Image of Africa: British Ideas and Action, 1780-1850, London, University Tutorial Press, p. 14, Wadström, op. cit., vol 2, p. 228

14. Wadström, op. cit., vol 1, pp. 94-95

15. Lorimer, D. (1978), Colour, Class and the Victorians, Leicester University Press, Holmes and Meier Publishers, Inc., passim

16. Blackburn, R. (1988), The Overthrow of Colonial Slavery 1776-1848, London, Verso, p.103.

17. Ibid., p.114

18. Ibid., p.116

19. Fryer, op. cit., p. 195-196

20. Ibid., pp.200-201

21. Lorimer, op. cit., p. 27, after Norton, M. B. (1973), 'The fate of some black loyalists of the American Revolution', Journal of Negro History, vol. LVIII, p.416

22. St. James Old Registers, Baptisms, 1801-12, 283 Jam 1/1C, Liverpool City Record Office, 1 Jan, 1801

23. "Dicky Sam", op. cit., p.10, after Williamson's Advertiser 1766. Also Fryer, op. cit., p.59.

24. Williams, G., op. cit., p.475, after Williamson's Advertiser June 24th 1757. Also Fryer, op. cit., p.59.

25. St. James Old Registers, Baptisms, 1775-1813, 283 Jam 1/1A, Liverpool City Record Office, 27 July, 1775

26. Wadström, op. cit., vol 1, pp. 94-95

27. Fryer, op. cit., p.59

28. Law and Henfrey, op. cit., p.24

29. Ibid., p.25

30. Ibid., p.24-25

31. Curtin, P. (1965), The Image of Africa: British Ideas and Action 1780-1850, London, University Tutorial Press, pp. 343-344

32. Law and Henfrey, op. cit., pp. 24-25

33. Duffield, I. (1981) "The History of Blacks in Britain: History and the Historians", History Today September, 1981, p. 34

34. Curtin, op. cit., p.vi

35. Wadström, op. cit., vol 1, pp. 94-95

36. Law and Henfrey, op. cit., pp. 25

37. File, N. and Power, C. (1986), Black Settlers in Britain 1555-1958, London, Heinemann, p. 27

38. Ustinov, P. (1977), Dear Me!, London, Mandarin, passim.

The Early History of Britain's Oldest Black Community

CHAPTER TWO

VISITORS AND SETTLERS

1   Wadström, op. cit., vol.2, p.319.

2.   Ibid., p.310.

3.   Ibid., p.269.

4.   Ibid., p. 270.

5.   Ibid., p.270.

6.   Fyfe, C. (1962) A History of Sierra Leone, London, Oxford University Press, p. 10.

7.   Wadström, op. cit., vol.2, p.75.

8.   Ibid., p.84.

9.   Ibid., p.320.

10.   Ransford, op. cit., pp.64-65.

11.   Williams, G. 1897, pp. 536-538.

12.   Ibid., pp. 541-542.

13.   Ibid., pp. 548-549.

14.   Shaw, G. T. (1907) Liverpool's First Directory, reprinted 1987, Scouse Press, Liverpool,p.60.

15.   Latham, A. J. H. (1973) Old Calabar 1600-1891: The Impact of the International Economy upon a Traditional Society, Clarendon Press, Oxford

16.   Priestley, op. cit., p.43.

17.   Ibid.

18.   Fryer, op. cit., p.423, after The Royal African: Memoirs of the Young Prince of Annomaboe, W. Reeve etc, c.1730, p.49

19.   St. James Old Registers, Baptisms 1775-1813, op. cit.

20.   Fyfe, C. op. cit., p. 10.

21.   Lorimer, op. cit., p.218.
22.   Fyfe, op. cit., p.217.

23.   Law, op. cit., p. 18.

CHAPTER THREE

EARLY LIVERPOOL-BORN BLACK PEOPLE

1.   St. James Old Registers, Baptisms, 1775-1813, op. cit.

2.   St. Nicholas' Baptismal Registers, 1796 Liverpool City Record Office.

3.   Faragher, M. (1995) "The Browns of the 'Times': an instance of Black social mobility in the 19th century" North West Labour History, Journal of the North West Labour History Group, Issue No. 20 - 1995/96, pp. 44-49.

4.   Lorimer. op. cit., p. 37.

5.   Ibid., p.39.

6.   Fryer, op. cit., p. 236, after Eifion, John Ystumllyn neu 'Black Jack',Tremadoc, R. Isaac Jones, 1888; reprinted Criccieth, Ngwasg y Castell, 1966.

7.   Ibid., p. 215.

8.   Ibid., p. 211.

9.   Fryer, op. cit., p. 216.

10.   Ibid., pp. 216-218.

11.   Ibid., p. 215.

12.   Ibid., p. 218.

13.   Duffield, I. (1981) "The History of Blacks in Britain: History and the Historians", History Today September, 1981, p. 34.

14.   Green, J. P. (1986) 'George William Christian: A Liverpool 'Black' in Africa', Transactions of the Historical Society of Lancashire and Cheshire, Vol. 134, p. 141-146.

15.   Marriage Certificate 22 Feb.,1873, Cert. No. 264, Liverpool Registrar of Births, Deaths and Marriages

16.   Marriage Certificate 24 Nov., 1853, Cert. No. 153, Liverpool Registrar of Births, Deaths and Marriages.

17.   Costello, R. (1995) "A Hidden History in Liverpool: The James Family", North West Labour History, Journal of the North West Labour History Group, Issue No. 20 - 1995/96, pp. 41-43.

18.   Creighton, S. (1995) "I am a Lancastrian bred and born...": The Life and Times of John Archer, 1863-1932", North West Labour History, Journal of the North West Labour History Group, Issue No. 20 - 1995/96,

105

pp. 73-85.

19. Law and Henfrey, op. cit., p. 7.

20. Dicky Sam, op. cit., p.51.

21. Law and Henfrey, op. cit., p. 25

22. Fryer, op. cit., p.290.

23. Ibid., p.295-296.

24. Birth Certificate, 24 Dec. 1914, Cert. No. 3, Liverpool Registrar of Births, Deaths and Marriages.

25. O'Mara, 1934, p. 221, as quoted in Law and Henry, op. cit., p.29.

26. Marke, E. (1986) In Troubled Waters, London, Karia Press, pp. 24-25

CHAPTER FOUR

SOCIAL CHANGE IN THE EIGHTEENTH AND NINETEENTH CENTURIES

1. St, James Old Registers 1801-1807, 1/1c p.1.

2. St. James Old Registers, Baptisms, 1775-1813, 283 Jam 1/1A, Liverpool City Record Office.

3. Lorimer, op. cit., p. 43.

4. Law and Henfrey, op. cit., p.30.

5. Frazer, W. M. (1947) Duncan of Liverpool, London, Hamish Hamilton Medical Books, p. 56.

6. Murphy, J. (1966) "The Rise of Public Elementary Education in Liverpool: Part Two, 1819-35", Transactions of the Historic Society of Lancashire and Cheshire, Vol. 118, Liverpool, printed for the Society, p. 121.

7. Lorimer, op. cit., p.27.

8. Newman, A. (Ed.) (1975) Liverpool, Provincial Jewry in Victorian Britain, London, Jewish Historical Society of England, p.1.

9. Lorimer, op. cit., p.27.

10. Moore, D. C. (1976) The Politics of Deference, New York, The Harvest Press, pp. 371-374.

11. Ibid.

12. Vallance, E. (1973/74) "An Interpretation of the Language of Justification in Nineteenth Century Educational Reform", Curriculum Network 3, Ontario Institute for Studies in Education, passim.

13. Swann Report, op. cit., p. 201.

14. Lorimer, op. cit., p.41.

15. Clerk, A. (1971) Arab - A Liverpool Street Kid Remembers, Liverpool, James E. James, p.26.

16. The Porcupine, July 20, 1861, No. XL., p.187

17. (1896) The Sunday at Home, 56 Paternoster Row, London EC, The Religous Tract Society, p. 308.

18. Holy Trinity, Parliament Street and Holy Trinity (Church of England) Schools, Ashwell Street, Toxteth, 18 vols., 1859-1941, Liverpool City Records 283 TRI Acc. 2506.

19. Ibid.

20. Dickens, C. (1898) The Uncommercial Traveller, London, Chapman and Hall, p.54, also quoted in Law and Henfrey, op. cit., p.20

21. Ibid., p.53. also quoted in Law and Henfrey, op. cit., p.20

22. Lorimer, op. cit., p.165

23. Cowper, A. (1948) A Backward Glance at Merseyside, Birkenhead, Wilmer Bros. & Co., p.31.

24. Law and Henfrey, op. cit., p.20.

25. Curtis, S. J. (1965) History of Education in Great Britain, London, p. 232.

26. Ibid.

27. Birkbeck Nevins, J. M.D. (1902) Liverpool Past and Present (A paper read before the Liverpool Geographical Society), December 4th, Picton Library, Liverpool, pp. 47-49.

28. Murphy, op. cit., p.108.

29. Ibid., p. 114.

30. Wood, J. W. (1920) unpublished manuscript, Harrington C. P. School, Stanhope Street, Liverpool 8.

31. O,Mara, P. (1934) The Autobiography of a Liverpool Slummy, Liverpool, Martin Hopkinson, p.74

32. (1896) "Sunday in Liverpool", a chapter in The Sunday at Home, The Religious Tract Society, 56 Paternoster Row, London EC, pp, 441-442.

33. Ibid.

34. Ibid.

35. Ibid.

36. O'Mara, (1934), also quoted in Law and Henry, op cit., p.29.

CHAPTER FIVE

THE CONSOLIDATION OF RACISM

1. The Rev. C. G. Moore, (1897) William Taylor of California: Bishop of Africa: an Autobiography, London, Hodder and Stoughton, 27 Paternoster Row, p. 387.

2. Coleridge-Taylor, A. (1979) The Heritage of Samuel Coleridge-Taylor, London, Dennis Dobson, p. 96; also Fryer, op. cit., p.259.

3. Fryer, op. cit., p. 296.

4. Gilbert, B. B. (1980) Britain Since 1918 , London, Billing and Son Ltd., p.30.

5. Ibid., p.28.

6. Fryer, op. cit., p.298.

7. Ibid., p.299.

8. Law, op. cit., p.30.

9. Fryer, op. cit., p. 301.

10. Ibid., p. 291

11. Ibid., p. 410

12. Ibid., p.415

13. Ibid., p.315

14. Little, K. (1972) Negroes in Britain , London, Routledge and Kegan Paul, p.82.

15. Law and Henfrey, op. cit., p.24,

16. Little, op. cit., p.83.

17. Ibid., p.84.

18. Ibid., pp. 87-88.

19. The Keys, p.4, as quoted in Little, op. cit., p.97

CHAPTER SIX

THE BLACK SETTLEMENT AREA

1. Cotton, V.E. (1951) The Story Of Liverpool, Liverpool, Liverpool City Council, pp. 10-11

2. Williams, G. op. cit.,

3. Wakefield MS, pp. 37-38

4. Frazer, W. M. (1947) Duncan of Liverpool, London, Hamish Hamilton Medical Books, p. 16

5. Williams, G., op. cit., p.303

6. Frazer, op. cit., p.57

7. Forwood, W. (1910) Recollections of a Busy Life, Liverpool, Henry Young & Sons, p. 10

8. Uduku, O. and Ben-Tovim, G. (1997) Social Infrastructure Provision in Granby /Toxteth , Liverpool, University of Liverpool, pp.5-6

9. Ibid.

10. Ibid.

11. Law, op. cit.,   p. 18

12. Frazer. op.cit., p.24.

13. Ibid. p. 18.

14. Ibid.

15. Ibid., p.43

16. Ibid., p. 79

17. (July 20, 1861) No. XL, "Sunday Evening in the Park", The Porcupine,   Porcupine Papers, Liverpool City Records Office, Hq 050 POR, p.187

18. Frazer, op. cit., p. 25-26

19. Uduku, O. and Ben-Tovim, G., op. cit, p.11

20. Ibid., pp. 11-12

21. Ibid.

22. Shepperson, G. (1983) "An early African Graduate" in Donaldson (ed.) Four Centuries, Edinburgh, University of Edinburgh, p. 92

23. Taylor, M. (1987/88) Worlds Apart, Windsor, N.F.E.R.-

Nelson, p. 336

24. Little, op. cit., p.214

25. Fryer, , op. cit., p.438 after Harlan, 1965, p.464

26. Uduku, O. and Ben-Tovim, G., op. cit., p. 14.

27. Ibid.

28. Ibid., p.13

CHAPTER SEVEN
FRIENDS AND ALLIES

1. Fryer, op cit, flyleaf

2. Law and Henfrey, op. cit. p. 14.

3. Lorimer p. 1978, 39-40.

4. Ibid..

5. Marke, E. (1986) In Troubled Waters, London, Karia Press, pp. 30-31

6. Williams, G. op. cit., pp. 577-578.

7. Gratus, J (19730) The Great White Lie, London, Hutchinson, p.67.

8. Fyfe, op. cit., p. 77.

9. Lorimer, op. cit., p. 32.

10. Fryer, op cit, p.77.

11. Lorimer, op cit, pp 33-34.

12. Ibid.

13. Third Annual Report of the Harrington Free School for the Education of Poor Children in Toxteth Park, May 5th, 1818

14. Murphy, 1964, p. 106.

15. Williams, G., op cit, p. 570.

16. Ibid.

17. Wood, J. W. (c.1926) Unpublished MS, Harrington C. P. School, p.2.

18. Williams, G. op. cit., p, 569.

19. Ibid. pp. 575-576

20. "Dicky Sam", op. cit. flyleaf .

21. Gordon and Lawton, op. cit., p.49.

22. Ibid.

23. Ibid.

24 Ibid, p. 232 .

25. Nevins, 1902, pp 47-49.

26. Murphy, 1964, p. 108.

27. Ibid, p.110.

28. Ibid, p.111.

29. Ibid., p.114.

30. Ibid, pp.115-116.

31. Ibid, p.125.

32. Ibid, p.132

33. Woodson, 1933, pp. 266-267.

34. O'Mara, op cit, p.74, also Law and Henfrey, op cit, p.27.

35. Law and Henfrey, op cit, p.27.

36. Fryer, op cit, p.294.

37. St. James Old Registers, Baptisms, op. cit., folio 1.

38. Law and Henfrey. op. cit., p.19.

39. H. Melville, 1849, p. 202, also quoted in Law, op. cit., p. 15.

40. July, R. W. (1968) The Origins of Modern African Thought, London, Faber and Faber, pp. 461-462.

41. Eugenics Review, Vol. XII, 1920-21, pp 76-77.

42. Ibid., p. 76-77.

43. Ibid., p. 69.

44. O'Mara, 1934, p.11, also Law and Henfrey, op. cit., p.25.

CONCLUSION

1. Norton, B. The Borrowers, 1952, passim.

2. Swann Commission, op. cit., p.192.